Pre-Civil War
Black Nationalism

Joseph Cinque: Heroic slave leader of the successful
rebellion aboard the slave-ship Amistad in 1839. The
ship's crew and captain were killed and all slaves (54)
were set free.

PRE-CIVIL WAR
BLACK NATIONALISM

by Bill McAdoo

The David Walker Press
New York

First Printing March 1983

Library of Congress Cataloging in Publication Data
LC Number: 83-60956

Published by The David Walker Press
P.O. Box 741, Brooklyn, New York 11207

ISBN: 0-912135-00-X (paperback)
ISBN: 0-912135-01-8 (hardbound)

PRINTED IN THE UNITED STATES OF AMERICA

Introduction To
Pre-Civil War Black Nationalism

Bill McAdoo's *Pre-Civil War Black Nationalism* is one of the most important studies of that period of U.S. history I've come across. Fundamentally, because it illuminates a key era in American life and particularly from the standpoint of African American history.

It is also written from the point of view of a progressive black activist-scholar during a period of upsurge in the Black Liberation Movement (1964) as well as the workers' and other national movements, and is obviously meant to provide not only an academic and historic framework to better understand the period but a guide to actively demarcate ideological development within the black national movement, as a guide to action.

The pre-civil war period is one of the most significant periods of U.S. history. It is the period of an intensification of slavery as it was transformed from feudalist patriarchal slavery to capitalist slavery. The slave was now not only tied to the land forever, but also a worker expected to produce a certain amount of cotton for an international market, and therefore more often "worked to death." Cotton had become more profitable on a world market so slavery got worse, even the few rights of the "free" blacks were called into question.

For this reason it is also a period of increased resistance by African Americans (both slave and free) to the slavery/white supremacy system. African American literature, as a genre, has its origins now, as the slave narratives, Douglass, Box Brown, Bibb, Roper, Brent, The Krafts, Wells Brown, Pennington, Stroyer, and the others fired powerful salvos against slavery with their accounts of black slaves oppressed, accommodating, defiant, fighting back, fleeing.

The slave narrators were the front line agitators who further motivated the free blacks of the north, who were also firing their own blasts aimed at destroying the hated institution. It was these free blacks who mainly participated in the *Black Convention Movement* that gathered black people and their allies to discuss how slavery might be destroyed and democracy won for African Americans.

McAdoo focuses with great clarity particularly on the ideological struggles that arose among these northern free blacks, showing us how the fundamental ideological groupings that developed then not only spoke to developing classes within an African American nationality, but also that these ideological groupings are still with us today. His basic defining of three trends "Stay & Fight"; "Submit" or "Black Zionism" is brilliant and is a breakdown and demarcation I never fail to point out to students and to send them to McAdoo's work itself. Unfortunately, till now, this remarkable little book has been unavailable (suffering the same fate as most black literature of all periods).

And if we will look at it, even today we are faced with the same three major tendencies within the black national movement. Stay and Fight is the ideology of the black masses, submission is the ideology of the accommodationist negroes among us, media and government appointed mis-leaders who tell us, "Hey, it ain't bad as it could be." McAdoo shows us they said it even during slavery! And the Black Zionists who still talk about returning to Africa, liquidating not only black struggle in the U.S. but the existence of the African American people themselves!

McAdoo shows us and analyzes the Abolitionist movement, the American Colonization Society (and the blacks sympathetic to it), makes clear the difference between the revolutionary sector of the black national movement, the Black Liberation Movement, and the reactionary nationalists of all stripes. He also discusses the great leaders of the period, Cinque, Garnett, Nat Turner, Denmark Vessey, Remond, C.H. Langston, David Walker and Douglass and the others. It is a portrait of an era, and of a struggling people in transition to even greater struggle. For anyone attempting to understand black ideological and organizational development just prior to the Civil War (which remains the most critically important period in U.S. history and the fundamental shaper of what U.S. society remains today) McAdoo's book is must reading! It should be on every bibliography of 19th century and Civil War courses given in Black Studies, American History or Political Science departments.

And certainly anyone wishing to understand more clearly the overall historical ideological development within the African American Nation and the Black Liberation Movement cannot do without this singular work.

Amiri Baraka,
Assoc. Professor,
Africana Studies
SUNY, Stony Brook
December 1982

"The colored people are not yet known, even to their most professed friends among the white Americans; for the reason, that politicians, religionists, colonizationists, and Abolitionists, have each and all, at different times, presumed to *think* for, dictate to, and *know* better what suited colored people, than they knew for themselves; and consequently, there has been no other knowledge of them obtained, than that which has been obtained through these mediums. Their history—past, present, and future, has been written by them, who, for reasons well known, which are named in this volume, are not their representatives, and, therefore, do not properly nor fairly present their wants and claims among their fellows. Of these impressions, we design disabusing the public mind, and correcting the false impressions of all classes upon this great subject. A moral and mental, is as obnoxious as a physical servitude, and not to be tolerated; as the one may, eventually, lead to the other...."

Martin R. Delany, 1852—black nationalist leader and theoretician

Pre-Civil War
Black Nationalism

The Origins of Black Nationalism Revolutionary and Reactionary

Afro-American nationalism has deep roots in the historical existence of the black masses in this country. Afro-American history has generally been disfigured, perverted, or concealed by the white rulers of America. And the story of the evolution of black nationalism, which forms an integral and organic part of Afro-Amcrican history as a whole, has suffered an even worse fate in the hands of the oppressor. The reasons for this can be simply stated and adequately proven.

First of all, it is within the wide embrace of Afro-American nationalism that we find the truly revolutionary traditions of black people prior to the Civil War. Secondly, without a fundamental understanding of thcsc black revolutionary traditions, it is impossible to chart a correct course for black liberation today. These black revolutionary traditions are, therefore, dangerous to the rich white imperialists who maintain Afro-Americans in a state of captivity and super-exploitation.

Black school children cannot find the story of these revolutionary traditions in their textbooks. Instead, they are fed a steady dict of traitors and collaborators like Booker T. Washington and others. Once the eyes ol the black masses are opened to their truc revolutionary traditions, they will be armed with an ideological weapon capable of laying the foundation for a revolutionary struggle for black liberation.

There are a wide variety of philosophical and political tendencies which have traditionally been called *black nationalism.* Nevertheless, a disciplined examination shows that there are ultimately and fundamentally only two brands of black nationalism: one is *revolutionary* in essence, while the other is *reactionary.* What appears to be a multiplicity of black nationalist philosophical and political tendencies boils down to a variation (or eclectic combination) of either the revolutionary or reactionary theme. Revolutionary nationalism has always advanced the struggle for black liberation while *reactionary nationalism has always tended to retard and subvert this struggle.*

The simple-minded, who have been brainwashed into accepting a stereotyped view of black nationalism as being a doctrine of black supremacy, race hatred, etc., have much to learn. For while they have identified some of the more obvious superficial characteristics of certain varieties of modern reactionary nationalism, they are totally blind to the fundamental precepts and historical role of revolutionary nationalism. Therefore, they compound their ignorance by painting *all* nationalists and *all* nationalism with the same brush, and they are totally unprepared to understand the role that black revolutionary nationalism will play in the struggle for black liberation today.

We are explicitly concerned, in the present documentary study, with the rise of Afro-American nationalism between 1830 and 1860 (pre-Civil War black nationalism). In the course of this study, both the revolutionary and reactionary varieties

African chief sells prisoners of war to European slave merchants.

2

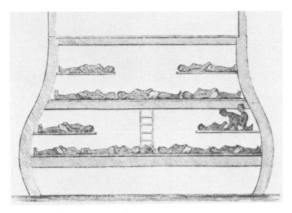

Cross section of a slave ship. Crowded, unsanitary conditions, and the absence of sufficient food and water, took a heavy toll of African lives.

of black nationalism will be defined by documentary example. But first, we must establish a historical perspective in order to place these documents in their proper context.

HISTORICAL BACKGROUND

The first African slaves were brought to the North American continent in 1619. Slavery in the other parts of the Americas, however, preceded North American slavery. Authorities estimate that during the entire course of the African slave trade, Africa lost nearly 50 million inhabitants, in order that the European and American slaveholders might secure 10 million slaves.[1] This was due to the fact that for every African slave successfully transported to the New World, four or five met death in numerous resistance wars, during the cruel forced marches from the interior of Africa to the coast, or during the horrors of middle passage on slave ships. This was the rape of Africa.

Among the diverse range of African peoples brought to North America from 1619 until the end of the American slave trade were Gaboons, Eboes, Congoes, Angolas, Senegalese, Coromantees, Whydahs, Nagoes, Paw Paws and others. These African peoples spoke different languages, were at different

3

stages of economic development, held different customs, embraced different religions and displayed a diverse range of physical characteristics. They were by no means *one* people with *one* common history. They had cultural characteristics and histories which were just as diverse and varied as the peoples who inhabit Europe or the peoples who came together to constitute what is today called white America.

It was during the course of enslavement in North America that the African slaves became one people with one history and one destiny. Slavery was its own *melting pot* and all of the diverse characteristics of the different African peoples who were enslaved were either intermingled, or systematically destroyed (as in the case of their languages). They became a people who shared a common form of oppression in a common slave economy. They came to speak a common language and to share a common national character; this transformation was completed long before the Civil War.

Needless to say, the African slaves were *not* "melted" into America, as was the case of the different European peoples who emigrated as free men, and who comprise what is now white America. Notwithstanding the acquisition of a common language, the African slaves were *kept out* of the melting pot (so to speak) which was to produce the white America of today. The history of black America is *not* identical to the history of white America even though there is an organic developmental relationship between the two. The history of the oppressed is never identical to the history of the oppressor: the history of the slaveholder can never be the same as the history of the slave. The history of black America began in Africa, while the history of white America began in Europe. The various European emigres who arrived in North America as free men eventually formed one people. The different African peoples who were brought here in chains grew to become another separate captive people, upon whose back America was built from its inception.

ORIGIN OF 'FREE' BLACKS
BEFORE THE CIVIL WAR

A small community of free black people existed during the entire course of slavery in America. These black people

Chart Number 1
COMPARISON BETWEEN BLACK POPULATION AND
TOTAL AMERICAN POPULATION
by numbers: 1800-1860

Census Year	Total U.S. population (black and white)	Total black population	Black percentage of total population
1800	5,308,483	1,002,037	19
1810	7,239,881	1,377,808	19.2
1820	9,638,453	1,771,656	18.5
1830	12,886,020	2,328,642	18
1840	17,069,453	2,873,648	16.9
1850	23,191,876	3,638,808	15.8
1860	31,443,321	4,441,830	14.1

NOTE

Between 1820 and 1860, 5 million whites emigrated to the United States, thus accounting for almost 25 percent of the total U.S. population increase for that period.

acquired their freedom by escaping and becoming fugitives, by buying their freedom, by gaining their freedom as a result of heroic service during the American Revolutionary War of 1776 and, in a very few cases, by voluntary manumission on the part of a few slaveholders. We have provided charts (1 and 2) to show both the numerical relationship of free blacks to slaves and the relationship of the total black population to the rest of the American population for the historical period under consideration.

In 1790 there were 59,577 free black people, 35,000 of whom lived in the South. By 1860, there were 488,070 free black people, 250,787 of whom lived in the South. (This may come as a shock to those who believe that the North was *the land of the free.*) During the entire course of slavery, the majority of free black people lived in the South. But a comparison of the condition of free blacks in the South with those in the North will demonstrate that there is no cause for shock. North or South, the free blacks were outcasts and little better than *free slaves.*

Free blacks in the North were kept out of the workshops (factories) and they were brutally discriminated against economically, politically and socially. There were few economic

5

Chart Number 2
BLACK POPULATION: Free and Slave, 1800 to 1860

Census Year	Slaves	Free blacks	Free black percentage of total
1800	893,602	108,435	10.8
1810	1,191,362	186,466	13.5
1820	1,538,022	233,634	13.2
1830	2,009,043	319,599	13.7
1840	2,487,355	386,293	13.4
1850	3,204,313	434,495	11.9
1860	3,953,760	488,070	11

Source: *Historical Statistics, Colonial Times to 1957.* Also see, *Statistical Abstract of the United States 1963* (pages 5 and 99) and *The Negro in Our History*, Woodson and Wesley (page 245).

opportunities open to them and the vast majority were either destitute or engaged in menial labor (house servants, etc.). The vast majority of northern free blacks were either directly prohibited from voting by law or prevented from voting because of property requirements and poll taxes.

All northern free blacks were excluded from juries, barred from public education (with a few exceptions), even though they were forced to pay education taxes. In addition, they had few rights that a white man was bound to respect. Fundamentally, as a point of comparison, the pre-Civil War North treated the black man as badly or worse than he is treated in the South today.

On the positive side, black people in the North did have freedom of speech, press and assembly. Moreover, they could even secure an education (by hook or crook) if they had enough money.

A small black middle class arose on top of the northern free black population. This was a class of small merchants and professional men. The story of the brilliant achievements of black scientists, doctors, lawyers, writers, inventors, etc. (against unbelievable odds) during the period of slavery in America is outside the bounds of this study, but the record of their achievements has been covered by Carter G. Woodson and other black historians.

Economically, free blacks in the South fared much better than those in the North. A considerable number were engaged as mechanics and artisans. They were preferred, not only because of their skill, but because they could be more easily exploited than the white worker. The free black man in the South had no rights that a white man was bound to respect; therefore he was constantly being cheated with no recourse to law. He was totally dependent. Nevertheless, it is remarkable to observe that in the South, with its predominantly agrarian slave economy, the free blacks were preferred as mechanics, artisans, tailors, shoemakers, etc., whereas in the industrial North the free blacks were excluded from the workshops. In the South, the bastion of slavery, it was easier for a black man to become a worker than in the industrial North (home of *free labor*) where black men were excluded from the workshops and forced to become house servants or perform other menial tasks.

On the negative side, a free black man in the South could be taken into custody and sold back into slavery if he were found to be without means of support or if he committed minor infractions of the law. There were a multitude of laws under which a black man could receive corporal punishment for crimes for which a white man would not even receive a fine. Black men could not testify against white men, nor could black men testify in their own behalf; they were absolutely excluded from juries and from voting and were barred from public education.

Moreover, there was no freedom of speech, press or assembly for free blacks in the South. In many cases a black man was required to show his "free papers" as a passport before he could move from one county to another or from one state to another in the South. Many southern states would not let a free black man return after he left the state, for fear that he might have been "corrupted" by contact with northern free blacks.

For those who are amazed that black men could be sold back into slavery in the South for paupery or minor infractions of the law, it might be well to remember that in 1849 a law was in force in the state of Ohio stating specifically that any black man who could not put up a bond of $500.00 was to be declared a pauper and sent to the workhouse! *There were no such laws for white men.* White immigrants without a penny to their names

7

could settle in the northern state of Ohio while black men were forced to post a $500.00 bond or go to jail; and Ohio was not the only northern state which indulged in such practices.

The small, southern black middle class was economically stronger and wealthier than the northern black middle class. A large section of the southern black middle class openly collaborated with the slaveholders and was able to win all sorts of special favors and considerations. In 1830, 3,777 black heads of families were reported to the United States Bureau of the Census as slaver owners.[2] Most of these black slaveholders lived in Louisiana, Maryland, North and South Carolina and Virginia.

A few of these black slaveholders had as many as from 50 to 200 slaves and held property to boot. They bought and sold slaves and lived in a state of luxury that was imitative of the white slave masters. Even though the black slave masters were a drop in the bucket as compared to the dominant white slaveholding South, their treachery stands as an important lesson to black people who wish to know the origin of present-day traitors. Booker T. Washington might well have been a black slave master had he been born a few years earlier.

Free blacks in the South had many contacts with the slaves. There were even marriages between free blacks and slaves, not to speak of the many slave revolts and conspiracies that were participated in and sometimes led by free blacks in the South.

BLACK POLITICAL ORGANIZATION

It was in the North, where free blacks did at least have the right to assemble, speak and publish, that we find a multitude of black organizations during the period under consideration (1830-1860). It is only natural, then, that the documentation which will be presented in this study of black nationalism originated from the northern free black population.

From 1830 until 1850 there were at least seven *National Negro Conventions* which took place exclusively in the North: 1830, 1831, 1832, 1833, 1834, 1835 and 1853. In addition, there were numerous *State Negro Conventions* in the North during this same period of time.

These conventions took place exclusively in the North and, with a few exceptions, the representatives were all from the free black population in northern states. Moreover, these representatives were members of the northern free black middle class. There is cause to wonder why the *National Negro Conventions* assumed such an imposing title since those present represented only the black population residing in the North, which was only 5 per cent of the total black population in America during this period. It would be more accurate to observe that these "national" conventions represented the deliberations and aspirations of sections of the northern free black middle class. This is precisely why these conventions are of immense importance to this study. The chief black nationalist spokesmen of this period were members of this same small, northern black middle class which participated in these conventions. We wish to contrast the political position taken by the nationalists with the predominant political position taken by these conventions.

We must state at the outset: the *National Negro Conventions* were managed and manipulated at the top by white liberals and moderates who were present at the conventions. These white liberal managers, who were called "philanthropists" by the black convention representatives, also formed the leading core of the white-controlled, so-called *Abolitionist movement* which also sprang up in the 1830's.

Delegates attend one of the pre-Civil War black conventions.

A white Abolitionist minister of New Haven, the Rev. S.S. Jocelyn, was one of the main "engineers" of the *First Annual Negro Convention of 1831*. Among other whites also present at the convention were W.L. Garrison, Arthur Tappan, and Benjamin Lundy. The following excerpts from the convention address will give some insight as to the role of these white "philanthropists."

"...Oh, then, by a brother's love, and by all that makes man dear to man—awake in time! Be wise! be free! Endeavour to walk with circumspection; be obedient to the laws of our common country; honour and respect its lawmakers and lawgivers; and, through all, let us not forget to respect ourselves.

"During the deliberations of this Convention, we had the favour of advising and consulting with some of our most eminent and tried philanthropists—men of unblemished character and of acknowledged rank and standing. Our sufferings have excited their sympathy; our ignorance appealed to their humanity; and, brethren we feel that gratitude is due to a kind and benevolent Creator, that our excitement and appeal have neither been in vain. A plan has been proposed to the Convention for the erection of a College for the instruction of young men of colour, on the manual labour system, by which the children of the poor may receive a regular classical education, as well as those of their more opulent brethren, and the charge will be so regulated as to put it within the reach of all. In support of this plan, a benevolent individual has offered the sum of one thousand dollars, provided that we can obtain subscriptions to the amount of nineteen thousand dollars in one year."[3]

The above excerpt speaks for itself. Black people are called upon to be obedient slaves. Moreover, there is no secret made of the guiding role played by the "eminent" white "philanthropists" during this Convention.

The white Abolitionists advocated a policy of *moral suasion* and *non-resistance* as the proper road for the black man to follow in his quest for liberation. This, of course, is the same path advocated by Martin Luther King. Non-resistance was the equivalent of what is called non-violence today.

John Brown. Black revolutionary nationalists like Dr. John S. Rock, saw John Brown as a man with whom they could identify. As reported in the *Liberator* of March 6, 1860, Dr. Rock characterized John Brown as the reincarnation of the black man who fell at the Boston Massacre, when he exclaimed that "John Brown of the second revolution is but Crispus Attucks of the first.

In short, the white Abolitionists were opposed to revolutionary struggle on the part of the black man. An exception to the rule was John Brown, a white *revolutionary* calling himself an Abolitionist but who clearly, in his deeds and words, believed that every true Abolitionist ought to be a revolutionary. John Brown's revolutionary course was opposed by almost all white Abolitionists.[4]

The *Second Annual National Negro Convention of 1832* again reflected the direct influence of these white liberal managers who called themselves Abolitionists. Here are a few excerpts from the convention address:

"We yet anticipate in the moral strength of this nation, a final redemption from those evils that have been illegitimately entailed on us as a people. We yet expect by due exertions on our part, together with the aid of the benevolent philanthropists of our country, to acquire a moral and intellectual strength, that will unshaft the calumnious darts of our adversaries, and present to the world a general character, that they will feel bound to respect and admire. . . .

"You there see that your country expects much from you and that you have much to call you into action, morally, religiously and scientifically. Prepare yourselves to occupy the several stations to which the wisdom of your country may promote you. We have been told in this Convention, by the Secretary of the American Colonization Society, that there are causes which forbid our advancement in this country, which no humanity, no legislation and no religion can control. Believe it or not. Is not humanity susceptible of all the tender feelings of benevolence? Is not legislation supreme—and is not religion virtuous? Our oppressed situation arises from their opposite causes. There is an awakening spirit in our people to promote their elevation, which speaks volumes in their behalf. We anticipated at the close of the last Convention, a larger representation and an increased number of delegates; we were not deceived, the number has been ten fold. And we have a right to expect that future Conventions will be increased by a geometrical ratio; until we shall present a body, not inferior in numbers to our state legislature, and the *phenomena* of an *oppressed people,* deprived of the rights of citizenship, in the midst of an enlightened nation, devising plans and measures for their personal and mental elevation, by *moral suasion alone.* . . .

"Be righteous, be honest, be just, be economical, be prudent, offend not the laws of your country—in a word, live in that purity of life, by both precept and example. . . ."[5]

The *National Negro Convention of 1853* gives us a clear insight concerning the one white liberal source of funds for the conventions.

The Harriet Beecher Stowe being referred to, in the following excerpt from the *Convention Call,* was the author of *Uncle*

Tom's Cabin:

"...Among the matters which will engage the attention of our Convention will be a proposition to establish a NATIONAL COUNCIL of our people with the view to permanent existence. The subject is one of vast importance, and should only be disposed of in light of a wise deliberation. There will come before the Convention matters touching the disposition of such funds as our friends abroad, through Mrs. Harriet Beecher Stowe, may appropriate to the cause of our progress and improvement. In a word, the whole field of our interests will be opened to enquiry, investigation and determination...."[6]

THE ABOLITIONIST MOVEMENT

The Abolitionist movement itself was a gathering place for all sorts of white political opportunists who were patently white supremacists. At a convention of the *New York Anti-Slavery Society*, held in Utica, September 20, 1837, a black minister, Reverend Theodore S. Wright, made a blistering speech against the predominant influence of opportunism and white supremacy in the Abolitionist movement.

"...Now a man may call himself an Abolitionist and we know not where to find him. Your tests are taken away. A rush is made into the abolition ranks. Free discussion, petition Anti-Texas, and political favor converts are multiplying. Many throw themselves in, without understanding the breadth and depth of the principles of emancipation. I fear not the annexation of Texas. I fear not all the machination, calumny and opposition of slaveholders, when contrasted with the annexation of men whose hearts have not been deeply imbued with these high and holy principles. Why, sir, unless men come out and take their stand on the principle of recognizing man as man, I tremble for the ark, and I fear our society will become like the expatriation society; everybody an Abolitionist....

"They lifted up their voices against slavery and the slave-trade. But, ah! with but here and there a noble exception, they go but half way. When they come to the grand doctrine, to lay the ax right down at the root of the tree, and destroy the very spirit of slavery—there they are defective. Their doctrine is to set the slave free, and let him take care of himself. Hence, we hear nothing about their being...viewed and treated according to their moral worth. Our hearts have recently been gladdened by an address of the Annual Meeting of the Friends' Society in the city of New York, in which they insist upon the doctrine of immediate emancipation. But that very good man who signed the document as the organ of that society within the past year, received a man of color, a Presbyterian minister, into his house, gave him his meals alone in the kitchen, and did not introduce him to his family. This shows how men can testify against slavery at the South, and not assail it at the North, where it is tangible...."[7]

THE AMERICAN COLONIZATION SOCIETY

The *American Colonization Society* was a white organization of slaveholders' representatives and representatives of northern capitalism dedicated to returning all free blacks to Africa. It had its beginnings in 1800, after the great black slave leader Gabriel Prosser staged an abortive insurrection in Virginia, which some authorities claim involved as many as fifty thousand black people. Slave revolts and conspiracies intensified enormously during the period of 1800 to 1860, and there is much solid historical evidence that free blacks were intimately involved in these revolts. During this period, free blacks in the South were being ruthlessly driven out. The slaveholders were becoming more and more desperate with each new revolt.

Free blacks who were forced out of the South poured into the North. The northern rulers were alarmed by the growing presence of free blacks in their domain and were just as determined to get rid of them as were the southern slaveholders. In 1800, immediately after Gabriel's revolt, the Governor of Virginia met with the President of the United States to take up the question of colonizing "persons obnoxious to the laws, or dangerous to the peace of society." The President, in turn, summoned Rufus King, who was then U.S. Ambassador to the English Court, and instructed him to ask the British if they would allow the U.S. to deport "undesirable" blacks to the British colony of Sierre Leone on the coast of Africa. These negotiations were fruitless because the British were having their own problems in this colony without the introduction of rebellious blacks.

The presence of free blacks was a constant danger to the institution of slavery. Not only did the number of slave rebellions intensify during the period of 1800 to 1860, but the number of escapes from slavery also mounted sharply. Along with this, political activity and organization among the free blacks of the North grew with amazing intensity from 1800 to 1860.

In 1816 a meeting was held in Washington which resulted in the formation of the *American Colonization Society*. Among those "great patriots" present at this meeting were Henry Clay, the compromiser; Francis Scott Key, the author of the *Star Spangled Banner*; John Randolph, a member of the United States Senate from Virginia; Judge Bushrod Washington, a brother of George Washington; Charles March, a Congressman from Vermont; Elijah H. Mills, a Congressman of Massachusetts; and Elisha B. Caldwell, Clerk of the United States Supreme Court.

Representatives of the *American Colonization Society* approached the U.S. government concerning the sending of free blacks to Africa. The matter was taken up by President Monroe and upon his recommendation it was agreed to purchase a small strip of territory on the Senegal River on the western coast of Africa. These racist hypocrites had the audacity to name this strip of land *Liberia* ("land of freedom") and to name its capital Monrovia in honor of President Monroe. A white Harvard professor, Professor Greenleaf, drew up a constitution for Liberia.

The territory finally brought under the control of Liberia was 43,000 square miles. This territory was annexed by force of arms. Both English and American ships and men participated in the killing of African tribesmen who resisted Liberia's encroachments upon their territory.

During the life of the *American Colonization Society,* only a few thousand free blacks were convinced to go to Liberia.

Colonization was resisted by the free black communities in the U.S. and the whole fraud was a flop.

Nevertheless, at its zenith, the *Colonization Society* sent agents throughout the country, spreading hatred for the black man. Even black agents were employed by the slaveholders and their northern cronies to do this dirty work. These black agents were usually members of the southern black middle class.

At this point it is important to note that Abraham Lincoln was one of the strongest advocates of colonization of the black man. His law emancipating the slaves of the District of Columbia, enacted April, 1862, provided $100,000 for the colonization of the black man. During the same year, he summoned a group of eminent black men before him and issued forth the following remarks:

> "... And, why should the people of your race be colonized and where? Why should they leave this country? You and we are different races. We have between us a broader difference than exists between almost any other two races. Whether it is right or wrong I need not discuss, but this physical difference is a great disadvantage to us both, as I think. Your race suffer very greatly, many of them, by living among us, while ours suffer from your presence. In a word we suffer on each side. If this is admitted, it affords a reason why we should be separated"—Abraham Lincoln, 1862[8]

These were the words of the *Great Emancipator* and if one cares to read either his *Emancipation Proclamation of 1863* or his other remarks about preserving the union *with* or *without* slavery, one can observe the true role of Lincoln as regards the black people. But he was not a hypocrite. He said what he meant. It is the white liberal hypocrites and their Uncle Tom flunkies of the present day who are attempting to pawn him off to the black people as a *great liberator*.

BLACK RESPONSE TO COLONIZATION

Typical of the responses from free blacks to the colonization menace are the following excerpts from an address by William Hamilton before the *Fourth Annual National Negro Convention*, held in New York in 1834:

Abraham Lincoln

"...But as long at least as the Colonization Society exists, will a Convention of coloured people be highly necessary. This society is the great Dragon of the land, before whom the people bow and cry, Great Jehovah, and to whom they would sacrifice the free people of colour. That society has spread itself over this whole land; it is artful, it suits itself to all places. It is one thing at the south, and another at the north; it blows hot and cold; it sends forth bitter and sweet; it sometimes represents us as the most corrupt, vicious, and abandoned of any class of men in the community. Then again we are kind, meek, and gentle. Here we are ignorant, idle, a nuisance, and a drawback on the resources of the country. But as abandoned as we are, in Africa we shall civilize and christianize all that heathen country. And by thus preaching continu-

17

ally, they have distilled into the minds of the community a desire to see us removed.

"They have resorted to every artifice to effect their purposes, by exciting in the minds of the white community, the fears of insurrection and amalgamation; by petitioning State legislatures to grant us no favours; by petitioning Congress to aid in sending us away; by using their influence to prevent the establishment of seminaries for our instruction in the higher branches of education...."[9]

When Governor Hunt of New York proposed, during his annual message to the Legislature (1852), that money be appropriated to advance the work of the *American Colonization Society,* an immediate response was evoked from the free black community in N.Y. *The New York State Convention of Colored Citizens of January 20, 1852,* went on record as follows:

"...*Thirdly*—We protest against such appropriation, because the American Colonization Society is a gigantic fraud...a moulder of, and a profiter by a diseased public opinion, it keeps alive an army of agents who live by plundering us of our good name.

"*And lastly*—We protest against this appropriation, because 'we remember those that are in bonds as bound with them'; bone of our bone and flesh of our flesh, may evil betide us when the hope of gain, or the fear of oppression, shall compel or persuade us to forsake them to the rayless gloom of perpetual slavery."[10]

BLACK CAPITALIST ASPIRATIONS

The free black middle class in the North lived in the heartland of northern capitalism. Most of these free blacks believed that only by developing a strong black capitalist economic base could they achieve final *liberation.* During a meeting in Boston, March 5, 1858, Dr. John S. Rock, a distinguished black physician and lawyer, stated the matter in the following manner:

"...In this country, where money is the great sympathetic nerve which ramifies society, and has a ganglia in every man's pocket, a man is respected in proportion to his success in business. When the avenues to wealth are opened to us, we will then become educated and wealthy, and then the roughest looking colored man that you ever saw, or ever will see, will be pleasanter than the harmonies of Orpheus, and black will be a very pretty color. It will make our jargon, wit—our words, oracles; flattery will then take the place of slander, and you will find no prejudice in the Yankee whatever. We do not expect to occupy a much better position than we now do, until we shall have our educated and wealthy men, who can wield a power that cannot be misunderstood. Then, and not till then, will the tongue of slander be silenced, and the lip of prejudice sealed. Then, and not till then, will we be able to enjoy true equality, which can exist only among peers."[11]

These black capitalist yearnings on the part of the northern black middle class were very concretely expressed at the many meetings and conventions which took place during the period of 1830 to 1860. The acquisition of capitalist means of production in both industry (workshops) and agriculture and the development of a black working class were specifically advocated. At the *State Convention of Ohio Colored Men,* held in Cincinnati, November 23-26, 1858, the following resolutions were among those adopted relating to developing a black capitalist base:

"...*Resolved* (4), That we say to those who would induce us to emigrate to Africa or elsewhere, that the amount of labor and self-sacrifice required to establish a home in a foreign land, would if exercised here, redeem our native land from the grasp of slavery; therefore we are resolved to remain where we are, confident that 'truth is mighty and will prevail.'

"*Resolved* (5), That we recommend to our people, in addition to the education they are so generally seeking to give their children, to train them in habits of useful industry.

"*Resolved* (6), That a combination of labor and capital will in every field of enterprise, be our true policy. Combination stores of every kind, combination workshops, and combination farms, will, if everywhere established, greatly increase our wealth; and with it our power...."[12]

The *National Negro Convention of 1853*, held in Rochester, New York, and attended by 114 delegates, established a detailed black economic program for achieving black capitalism. Among a wide range of measures, they called for the establishment of a "protective union" (sort of a "buy black" outfit), and a "Registry of Colored Mechanics, Artisans and Businessmen" to advance their black capitalist aspirations. Below are a few excerpts from the convention documents:

"...*Article 4*—The Committee on Protective Union shall institute a Protective Union for the purchase and sale of articles of domestic consumption, and shall unite and aid in the formation of branches auxiliary to their own.

"*Article 5*—The Committee on Business Relations, shall establish an office, in which they shall keep a registry of colored mechanics, artizans and business men throughout the Union. They shall keep a registry of all persons willing to employ colored men in business, to teach colored boys mechanical trades, liberal and scientific professions, and farming; and, also, a registry of colored men and youth seeking employment or instruction. They also shall report upon any avenues of business or trade which they deem inviting to colored capital, skill or labor. Their reports and advertisements to be in papers of the widest circulation. They shall receive for sale or exhibition, products of the skill and labor of colored people...

"...the following branches of industry: general smithing, turning, wheel-wrighting and cabinet-making; and a general work-shop in which may be combined such application of skill in wood, iron, and other material as to produce a variety of saleable articles with suitable buildings and machinery for producing the same. These superintended by competent workmen, under pay precisely as other teachers, would give students a foundation for after self-support in life, and break down the distinctions that never ought to exist between the study and the work-shop. The above industrial pursuits are named, not because others more desirable perhaps, or more difficult to secure, might not have had a place given them in this imperfect report; but, because it seemed wise to choose some which are primary to most others in general usefulness, and at the same time, such as whose products have an extensive marketable demand. In establishing workshops, it must be remembered that the introducing of any large part of the very useful or lucrative branches is an utter impossibility. All that can be aimed at in the beginning, is to elevate labor to its own true standard—vindicate the laws of physical health, and at the same time, as a repaying benefit, make the work done as intrinsic and *profitable....*"[13]

During the entire course of slavery in America, the free black middle class had been systematically excluded from the acquisition of capitalist means of production in industry and agriculture. Moreover, they had never been "integrated" into the fabric of northern capitalism. But, living in the midst of a white northern capitalist environment, they observed that under capitalism only those who had wealth and power could command their own destinies. The white American captains of industry and agriculture ruled the day and held command over the nation. The whites who lived within this capitalist arena enjoyed varying degrees of bourgeois democracy, depending upon what class they belonged to, while the slaves and free blacks, who were maintained on the outside in a state of national oppression, had neither capitalist means of production, nor wealth, nor national power, nor any of the benefits of bourgeois democracy. It is not difficult then to understand why the black middle class aspired to black capitalism.

Capitalism requires the concentration of a mass army of free wage laborers. The black middle class could not hope to fulfill their black capitalist aspirations while slavery and the Mason-Dixon line separated them from their potential source of black labor power. Also, the existence of slavery cramped their style in another way. In order to safeguard the enslavement of 90 per cent of the black population, the slaveholders and their northern capitalist allies had to reduce the remaining 10 per cent, who were nominally free, to a status of *free slaves.*

How could the oppressor in one instance make the free black man a citizen with full economic, social and political equality and, on the other hand, expect to maintain the vast majority of black men in a brutal, abject state of bond slavery? The mere existence of free blacks, even though they were no better than

21

free slaves, was antagonistic and contradictory to slavery. That the black middle class was amply aware of this contradiction is demonstrated in the following excerpts from the Convention Address of the *National Negro Convention,* held in Rochester, New York, 1853:

"...Now, what is the motive for ignoring and discouraging our improvement in this country? The answer is ready. The intelligent and upright free man of color is an unanswerable argument in favor of liberty, and a killing condemnation of American Slavery. It is easily seen that, in proportion to the progress of the free man of color in knowledge, temperance, industry, and righteousness, in just that proportion will he endanger the stability of slavery; hence, all the powers of slavery are exerted to prevent the elevation of the free people of color.

"The force of fifteen hundred million dollars is arrayed against us; hence, the press, the pulpit, and the platform, against all the natural promptings of uncontaminated manhood, point their deadly missiles of ridicule, scorn and contempt at us, on pain of being pierced through and through, to remain in our degradation.

"Let the same amount of money be employed against the interest of any other class of persons, however favored by nature they may be, the result could scarcely be different from that seen in our own case. Such a people would be regarded with aversion; the money-ruled multitude would heap contumely upon them, and money-ruled institutions would proscribe them. Besides this money consideration, fellow-citizens, an explanation of the erroneous opinions prevalent concerning us is furnished in the fact, less creditable to human nature, that men are apt to hate most those whom they injure most. Having despised us, it is not strange that Americans should seek to render us despicable; having enslaved us, it is natural that they should strive to prove us unfit for freedom; having denounced us as indolent, it is not strange that they should cripple our enterprise; having assumed our inferiority, it would be extraordinary if they sought to surround us with circumstances which would serve to make us direct contradictions to their assumption."[14]

Martin R. Delany, doctor, writer, and field officer in the Civil War.

BLACK ZIONISM

The dominant form of reactionary black nationalism, arising between 1830 and 1860, was *black zionism*. Martin R. Delany, a black writer, editor and theoretician, was one of the chief spokesmen and prime movers of black zionism. He set forth the black zionist doctrine very competently in his book, *The Condition, Elevation, Emigration and Destiny of the Colored People of the United States, Politically Considered* (published by the author in Philadelphia in 1852).

"...Every people should be the originators of their own designs, the projector of their own schemes, and creators of the events that lead to their destiny—the consummation of their desires.

"Situated as we are, in the United States, many, and almost insurmountable obstacles present themselves. We are four-and-a-half millions in numbers, free and bond; six hundred thousand free, and three-and-a-half millions bond.

"We have native hearts and virtues, just as other nations; which in their pristine purity are noble, potent, and worthy of example. We are a nation within a nation;—as the Poles in Russia, the Hungarians in Austria; the Welsh, Irish, and Scotch in the British dominions.

"But we have been, by our oppressors, despoiled of our purity, and corrupted in our native characteristics, so that we have inherited their vices, and but few of their virtues, leaving us in character, really a *broken people.*

"Being distinguished by complexion, we are still singled out—although having merged in the habits and customs of our oppressors—as a distinct nation of people; as the Poles, Hungarians, Irish and others, who still retain their native peculiarities, of language, habits, and various other traits. The claims of no people, according to established policy and usage, are respected by any nation, until they are presented in a national capacity.

"To accomplish so great and desirable an end, there should be held, a great representative gathering of the colored people of the United States; not what is termed a National Convention, representing en masse, such as have been, for the last few years, held at various times and places; but a true representation of the intelligence and wisdom of the colored freemen; because it will be futile and an utter failure, to attempt such a project without the highest grade of intelligence....

"To effect this, and prevent intrusion and improper representation, there should be a CONFIDENTIAL COUNCIL held; and circulars issued, only to such persons as shall be *known* to the projectors to be equal to the desired object.

"The authority from whence the call should originate, to be in this wise:—The originator of the scheme, to impart the contemplated Confidential Council, to a limited number of known, worthy gentlemen, who agreeing with the project, endorse at once the scheme, when

becoming joint proprietors in interest, issue a *Confidential Circular,* leaving blanks for date, time, and place of holding the Council, sending them to trusty, worthy and suitable colored freemen, in all parts of the United States, and the Canadas, inviting them to attend; who when met in Council, have the right to project any scheme they may think proper for the general good of the whole people—
. . .

"By this Council to be appointed, a Board of Commissioners, to consist of three, five, or such reasonable number as may be decided upon, one of whom shall be chosen as Principal or Conductor of the Board, whose duty and business shall be, to go on an expedition to the EASTERN COAST OF AFRICA,. . .

"The National Council shall appoint one or two Special Commissioners to England, France, to solicit in the name of the Representatives of a Broken Nation, of four-and-a-half millions, the necessary outfit and support, for any period not exceeding three years, of such an expedition. Certainly, what England and France would do, for a little nation—mere nominal nation, of five thousand civilized Liberians, they would be willing and ready to do, for five millions; if they be but authentically represented, in a national capacity. What was due to Greece, enveloped by Turkey, should be due to United States, enveloped by the United States; and we believe would be respected, if properly presented. To England and France, we should look for sustenance, and the people of those two nations—as they would have everything to gain from such an adventure and eventual settlement on the EASTERN COAST OF AFRICA—the opening of an immense trade being the consequence. The whole Continent is rich in minerals, and the most precious metals, as but a superficial notice of the topographical and geological reports from that country, plainly show to any mind versed in the least, in the science of the earth. . . The land is ours—there it lies with inexhaustible resources; let us go and possess it. In Eastern Africa must rise up a nation, to whom all the world must pay commercial tribute.

"We must MAKE an ISSUE, CREATE an EVENT,

and ESTABLISH a NATIONAL POSITION for OUR-
SELVES: and never may expect to be respected as men
and women, until we have undertaken, some fearless,
bold, and adventurous deeds of daring—contending
against every odds—regardless of every consequence."

The above excerpts from Delany's book contain the fundamental kernel of black zionism. Other black zionists, like H.
Ford Douglass (no relation to Frederick Douglass), whom we
will hear from later, further elaborated some of the specific
tenets of black zionism, but Delany's exposition presents a
more complete picutre of the fundamentals of this reactionary
brand of nationalism.

Black zionism had a dual character. It borrowed from revolutionary nationalism the concept of the black people comprising
a *nation within a nation*. It also borrowed from revolutionary
nationalism the fundamental concepts that the black nation
had a unique *national character* and that the sacred right of all
nations is the right of *self-determination*. Moreover, black zionists like Delany helped to raise some of these important concepts to their highest theoretical level. So, while they did not
originate these concepts, they nevertheless performed a service
of untold magnitude, by helping to elevate and elaborate them,
even though their purpose and designs for doing so were fundamentally reactionary and counter-revolutionary. This, in a
word then, captures the duality of black zionism.

Delany stated that the black people in the United States
constituted a *nation within a nation* and he gave valid examples
to support this view. Moreover, he observed that the black
nation was a captive nation like Ireland under the oppressive
yoke of Great Britain. Delany gave one of the most concise and
brilliant statements on the right and meaning of the self-
determination of nations: "Every people should be the originators of their own designs, the projector of their own schemes,
and the creators of the events that lead to their destiny—the
consummation of their desires."

Also, he asserted that the black people, even though they had
"merged" in the habits and customs of our oppressor—as a
distinct nation—retained their "native peculiarities, of language, habits, and various other traits" (i.e., national character)
in the same way that the Irish and other oppressed people (who

had merged in the habits and customs of their oppressors) retained their national character. To cap this off, Delany correctly stated, in effect, that no oppressed nation could be considered free until it attained its own government and its own sovereign state, or at least some "national capacity" which served to represent its interests.

It was the elaboration of concepts borrowed from black revolutionary nationalism which gave black zionism its nationalist character. Without this theoretical front it would be almost impossible to distinguish the black zionist program from that of the oppressor's *American Colonization Society*. Indeed, some black historians, like Carter G. Woodson, have preferred to call Martin R. Delany and his cohorts *colonizationists*. But such a characterization, while it is correct, tends to obscure the duality of black zionism, and while it serves to expose its fundamentally reactionary character, it also tends to deny the validity of the black zionist contributions to the theoretical study of the national question.

It is after consideration of the national question that the reactionary nature of black zionism is revealed. Delany and other black zionists called for the establishment of a black capitalist nation in Eastern Africa with a view to "possessing" and exploiting the entire continent of Africa. He definitely excludes the possibility of establishing a sovereign black state on the North American continent. Why was this a fundamentally reactionary course? The answer is simple, when one views the history and objective conditions of life of the black masses under slavery.

The black zionists believed, in effect, that slavery in America could not be overthrown. They did not believe in the revolutionary potential of the enslaved black masses, even though the multitude of slave revolts and the emergence of revolutionary nationalism gave irrefutable proof of this potential. In fact, the black zionists looked down upon the black masses (including the majority of poor free blacks) and argued that the destiny of the black nation could not be entrusted in their hands. Only "worthy gentlemen," only " trusty, worthy colored freemen" were capable of becoming "joint proprietors" in determining the destiny of the black nation. The class prejudices displayed by Delany were not alien to the black middle class of those times.

The facts are that there was no way in hell that the 90 per cent of the black masses who were slaves could leave North America while the power of the *slavocracy* was supreme. The only people that the black zionists could take to their "promised land" would have been the free blacks. The vast majority of the black masses would have been abandoned and surrendered to the oppressor. The black zionists believed that the power of the slaveholders could not be broken, so it is obvious that abandonment of the enslaved black masses was a necessary part of their scheme. They would in effect, help to make America safe for slavery, by siphoning off the free black population and preventing a united front revolutionary struggle for black liberation. Therefore, their fundamental role was almost exactly the same as the reactionary *American Colonization Society*. Is there any wonder that the black masses gave the same answer to the black zionists that they gave to the *American Colonization Society?*

No matter what reasons the black zionists gave to justify their plans, the fundamental fact is that they served the interests of the oppressor and not the interests of the enslaved black masses. But this is only the most obvious side of black zionism's reactionary nature.

The black zionists had designs on Africa, but they were not in the spirit of a "long lost" descendant returning to his ancestral home (after two centuries of oppression) to live among "his own" in peace and harmony. This was not their intention, nor was it possible. Africa was inhabited by many different tribes, who century after century had resisted internal and external encroachments. They had been enslaved by both blacks and whites. Therefore, the mere quality of being *black* was not a passport to special privileges in Africa. The Northern American blacks were just as much strangers to the Africa peoples as the white French and English. After 250 years of physical separation and separate historical development, the North American black had little in common with the various African peoples except for a common historical origin of ancestry. But the African peoples weren't reading history books that year. The various African tribesmen did not make special allowances for a person because he was black or because he had been wandering in the wilderness of oppression for 250 years.

28

Every inch of inhabitable land in Africa was either occupied or claimed by one of the many African peoples. Wars were fought to secure these claims because land was the foundation and lifeblood of each of the African cultures and societies. Therefore, "visitors who came to stay" were most unwelcome, and only superior force of arms and defeat in bloody battles could make these various African peoples surrender their lands. The black zionists knew this as well as anyone else. That is why they called upon England and France to extend the necessary "provisions" (including military aid, of course) to accomplish their plans for possessing and exploiting Africa. Their plan was one of conquest and exploitation.They were not returning to the "bosom of mother Africa" to rejoin the "tribe" after a long sojourn in the wilderness of oppression. They were returning to commit rape and incest. They were returning to possess and exploit Africa in accordance with their black capitalist aspirations.

Liberia provides us with a good example of this because not only did the black North Americans who ruled Liberia seize the land by force of arms (with the military aid of the Americans and the English), but they also enslaved various tribal peoples and forced them to work for them. The black Liberians were slaveholders, and there are many plantations in Liberia to this very day where the people are held in a virtual condition of slavery. Concerning this fact of history, the noted black historian, Carter G. Woodson, has said of Liberia: "Unfortunately those in control took their cue for the treatment of the natives from the slaveholders of the United States by whom their forebears were...sent to Africa."[15]

So the crimes that the white founders of the United States committed against humanity, namely, the extermination of the American Indians, the seizure of the land of the Indians, and the enslavement of Africans, were repeated on a smaller scale by the founders of Liberia and their white imperialist sponsors. The black zionists aspired to this same type of brutal, primitive capitalist accumulation. It was the logical extension of their doctrine. Africa was their "promised land" and Liberia was their model even though, for practical political reasons, they verbally disassociated themselves from the *American Coloniza-*

Dr. James McCune Smith   **John M. Langston**

tion Society and the American government which established Liberia. The capture and exploitation of African labor power and African resources, with the aid of the white imperialists, in order to fulfill black capitalist aspirations, were fundamental to black zionism. The black zionists believed in "deals at the top" with the imperialists. Those who had little faith in the revolutionary potential of the black masses put themselves under the wing of an imperialist sponsor, imitated the oppressor, and became tools of the oppressor. The black zionists took their cues from the most reactionary American traditions.

Have we not seen this happen in the recent past? If black zionists would have seized the territory which is now called Israel, after making a deal with the British, (who were interested in establishing a favorable balance of power), if black zionists would have displaced indigenous peoples, seized their lands, and carried on a vicious predatory war against them; would the victims of this infamy have looked the other way, simply because they were black or simply because they had been oppressed? Would the Egyptians, Syrians and the Jordanians have said: "Welcome! my land is your land. You've been gone so long, but now you're home. Good thing you're *black* or we would have been mad at you for killing our people, taking our land, etc." No, indeed! No, indeed! There would have been no welcome to the "promised land" on that day.

A word about Liberia. Liberia has never been free of white imperialist domination (usually through control of the economy). In the beginning, the U.S. Government and its *American Colonization Society* front envisaged Liberia as an American-controlled enclave (or foothold) in Africa. Later, Liberia fell to British domination, after which America moved back in on the wings of the multi-million dollar *Firestore Corporation,* which virtually controls all of the plantations in Liberia today. Could the black zionists of 1852 expect anything better than domination by the very imperialist powers to whom they looked for sponsorship? History proves otherwise. They would have just been part of France and England's over-all plans for the conquest of Africa.

H. FORD DOUGLASS

H. Ford Douglass (no relation to Frederick Douglass), native of Louisiana and noted black zionist cohort of Martin R. Delany, delivered a revealing address at the Emigration Convention at Cleveland, Ohio, on August 27, 1854. This address was a reply to J.M. Langston (brother of the revolutionary nationalist, C.H. Langston), who had spoken in opposition to the black zionist schemes for emigration. The reply was also aimed at Frederick Douglass and J. McCune Smith, who likewise had opposed the black zionists.

"...Because Mr. (Frederick) Douglass, Mr. (J. McCune) Smith or Mr. (J. Mercer) Langston tell me that the principles of emigration are destructive to the best interests of the colored people in this country, am I to act the part of a 'young robin,' and swallow it down without ever looking into the merits of the principles involved? No! Gentlemen. You must show some more plausible reason for the faith which is within you...

"Is not the history of the world, the history of emigration?... The coming in and going out of nations, is a natural and necessary result... Let us then be up and doing. To stand still is to stagnate and die... Shall we then refuse to follow the light which history teaches, and be doomed, like our 'fathers,' to perish in the dark wilderness of oppression?

"No! In spite of the vapid anathemas of 'Eastern Stars,' who have become so completely dazzled by their own supposed elevation, that they can scarcely see any of the dark realities below; or the stale commonplace of 'Western satellites' the expediency of a 'COLORED NATIONAL-ITY,' is becoming self-evident to Colored men more and more every day.

"It is not our 'little faith,' that makes us anxious to leave this country or that we do not believe in the ultimate triumph of the principles of FREEDOM, but that the life-sustaining resources which slavery is capable of commanding may enable the institution to prolong its existence to an indefinite period of time. You must remember that slavery is not a foreign element in this government nor is it really antagonistic to the feelings of the American people. On the contrary, it is an element commencing with our medieval existence, receiving the sanction of the early Fathers of the Republic, sustained by their descendants through a period of nearly three centuries, deep and firmly laid in our organization. Completely interwoven into the passions and prejudices of the American people. It does not constitute a local or sectional institution as the generous promptings of the great and the good (Charles) Sumner would have it, but is just as national as the Constitution which gives it an existence. . .

"I can hate this Government without being disloyal, because it has stricken down my manhood, and treated me as a saleable commodity. I can join a foreign enemy and fight against it, without being a traitor, because it treats me as an ALIEN and a STRANGER, and I am free to avow that should such a contingency arise I should not hesitate to take any advantage in order to procure indemnity for the future. . .

"When I remember that from Maine to Georgia, from the Atlantic waves to the Pacific shore, I am an alien and an outcast, unprotected by law, proscribed and persecuted by cruel prejudice, I am willing to forget the endearing name of home and country, and as an unwilling exile seek on other shores the freedom which has been denied me in the land of my birth."[16]

One of the key passages in Douglass' remarks contains the

concept that the "life-sustaining resources which slavery is capable of commanding may enable the institution to prolong its existence to an indefinite period of time." In other words, slavery was almost eternal. This notion parallels Delany's assertion that "insurmountable obstacles" stand in the way of black liberation on the North American continent. Douglass' estimate as to the national scope of slavery and the white supremist prejudices of the American people was totally valid. But even white supremists have been known to die when they were shot down. The slave revolts proved this. Self-interest and the necessities of survival have always proved more powerful in determining the actions of the oppressor, when the deal is down, than white supremist notions. The Civil War proved this. White supremacy is only a cover (a justification) for something which is in essence far more fundamental.

The Civil War was a conflict between northern capitalist white supremists and Southern slaveholding white supremists. And we can be sure that the freedom of the black man was not the issue. Even so, it afforded the black man a great opportunity to take advantage of this antagonistic division within the white American ruling class to fight in his own behalf. He pursued this opportunity heroically and magnificently. But the black man should have killed a few more on both sides. He should have prolonged the war in the South until every single slaveholder had been wiped out. In that way, the seeds that produced Senator Eastland, Senator Byrd, and Lyndon B. Johnson would have been snuffed out, and the black man would not have bestowed them on his posterity. The black man should have seized the land which belonged to him by force of arms. That way, the capitalist North would have had to use the Union Army to smash black Reconstruction, instead of employing its reconstituted slave-master flunkies. The black man would not have been any worse off. And there would probably be fewer brainwashed "Negroes" today.

On the other hand, if a black man had shot Lincoln, we would not have to see his picutre in our textbooks and on our school walls to remind us how "free" we are today. Then, instead of pretending to be our "friends," the white liberals of today would be saying: "Hark! We gave you a white Moses once, and just look what you done to him!"

33

In any case, the equation which H. Ford Douglass established between white supremacy and the impossibility of achieving black liberation was entirely false. Those who were willing to abandon the enslaved black masses to the whims and "mercies" of the oppressor, while they sought after immediate personal gain and glory in Africa, would have done more to prolong the agony of slavery than all the forces of white supremacy put together. What better way to justify a cowardly and opportunist policy than to call all other courses impossible and to call the enemy eternal? What better way to serve the enemy, while at the same time pretending to denounce him?

H. Ford Douglass asserted that the history of the world was "the coming in and going out of nations," in other words, the emigration of nations. Every student of history knows that this is a falsehood. Frederick Douglass placed the question in the following correct way: "Individuals emigrate—nations never." The Irish nation didn't cease to exist because individual Irishmen emigrated to America. The Easter Rebellion of 1916 and the guerilla war against the English oppressor in 1918 took place without them. England and all of the other nations from which individuals emigrated to the United States are still intact. Nor would the black nation in America cease to exist simply because a few black zionists, who called themselves "the nation," wanted to run away.

The schemes of the black zionists failed miserably. Even though they did send a few individuals to East Africa and other places to investigate the possibilities of establishing a "promised land," their plans flopped. Ironically enough, during the Civil War, H. Ford Douglass became a captain in the Kansas corps of the U.S. Army, while Martin R. Delany became a major in the U.S.C.T. One Hundred and Fourth Regiment. Perhaps they smelled the new possibilities of putting their black capitalist monkey on the backs of the black masses right here at home? We will have more to say about the black zionists after we review the documents and principles of revolutionary nationalism.

BLACK REVOLUTIONARY NATIONALISM

Black revolutionary nationalism was the most dynamic and, historically speaking, the most powerful and important political force to arise during the period under consideration (1830-1860). Its singular importance rests not in the measure to which it was or was not embraced, nor does it rest in a catalog of victories or defeats which may be associated with its emergence. Its greatness lies in the simple fact that it corresponded to the objective and subjective conditions of the times in which it was born. More plainly, in a situation which clearly demanded revolution, black revolutionary nationalism advanced and elaborated a correct revolutionary course. In a situation which demanded the national consolidation of the oppressed black masses into a revolutionary army for black liberation, only revolutionary nationalism advanced this policy. Black revolutionary nationalism depended entirely upon the proven revolutionary potential of the enslaved black masses as the one force capable of ultimately determining the course of black liberation. Unlike black zionism, reformism, or conservatism, revolutionary nationalis *did not* depend upon "deals at the top" or confinement within the bounds of the oppressor's "law and order" or faith in the oppressor's ultimate "moral goodness." It was founded upon the notion of the revolutionary overthrow of the oppressor, and the assertion of the rights of what they considered to be an oppressed black nation, in the same fashion that all other oppressed nations had achieved liberation throughout the course of history.

Their model was the American Revolutionary War of 1776. Their guiding principles were the same as those expounded in the Declaration of Independence and the various other documents which reflect the revolutionary character of that conflict. They adapted these principles and precepts to the special history and unique objective existence of the black people in America. They had no illusions about the American Revolutionary War of 1776. They knew that they had been excluded from its benefits. They knew that when the white slaveholding revolutionary leaders of that time said that "all men are created

35

equal," the black man was considered less than an animal and therefore to be excluded. But in a larger context the black revolutionary nationalists recognized the validity of the 1776 contest as an example to all oppressed nations seeking to throw off the yoke of an oppressor. Were they to reject the concept of revolution altogether, simply because the American revolutionaries were white supremist slaveholders and hypocrites? No, indeed! This would be like refusing to fire a gun at the slave-holding enemy simply because the gun is stamped *Made in U.S.A.* A gun is no respecter of colors, it doesn't care who pulls the trigger. The revolutionary nationalists believed that "liberty or death" was just as valid for the black man as for the whites.

It must be remembered that the American Revolutionary War of 1776 was a nationalist war. It was a war to secure self-determination for the American nation. It was a war of national liberation from the oppressive yoke of England. In those days, nationalism was called "patriotism." It had nothing to do with color because both of the adversaries were white. This patriotism was an expression of national pride, pride in a nation and its history. It was a patriotic war for national liberation, and this was the basis for its nationalist character. A flag was made to symbolize it, songs were written about it, and documents recording its history and development were assembled and preserved for posterity. A few more American Indians were slaughtered to celebrate it. And a few more black women were raped so that their offspring could walk and weep behind Abe Lincoln's casket in honor of it. (Some brainwashed blacks are still walking behind Abe's casket to this very day.)

The black revolutionary nationalists had a deep and abiding pride in their ancestral origins and history. They too were waging a struggle for national liberation, and the history of this struggle was written by the great slave revolts and their leaders. They were proud of the resistance put up by black men during their long captivity under the yoke of the oppressor. So, while they didn't murder American Indians to celebrate it, they displayed the national pride of an oppressed people determined to be free. These factors gave a nationalist character to their revolutionary struggle.

A scene from the Boston Massacre, showing British troops firing on a Boston mob led by runaway slave Crispus Attucks. A monument to Attucks and four other Revolutionary War heroes stands in Boston.

GARNET'S CALL TO REBELLION

Henry Highland Garnet may one day be recorded as the "young lion" of black liberation. In 1843, at the age of 27, he delivered a call entitled "An Address to the Slaves of the United States." It was first delivered at the *National Negro Convention* held in Buffalo, New York, August 21-24, 1843. It was subsequently printed and widely read. Over 71 delegates attended, and the address failed by only one vote to be adopted as the sentiment of the convention.

Garnet's *Call to Rebellion* is the very embodiment of revolutionary nationalism, as the following excerpts will demonstrate:

"... While you have been oppressed, we have also been partakers with you; nor can we be free while you are enslaved. We, therefore, write to you as being bound with you....

"Two hundred and twenty-seven years ago, the first of our injured race were brought to the shores of America. They came not with glad spirits to select their homes in the New World. They came not with their own consent, to find an unmolested enjoyment of the blessings of this fruitful soil. The first dealings they had with men calling themselves Christians, exhibited to them the worst features of corrupt and sordid hearts; and convinced them that no cruelty is too great, no villainy and no robbery too abhorrent for even enlightened men to perform, when influenced by avarice and lust. Neither did they come flying upon the wings of Liberty, to a land of freedom. But they came with broken hearts, from their beloved native land, and were doomed to unrequited toil and deep degradation. Nor did the evil of their bondage end at their emancipation by death. Succeeding generations inherited their chains, and millions have come from eternity into time, and have returned again to the world of spirits, cursed and ruined by American slavery....

"In a few years the colonists grew strong, and severed themselves from the British Government. Their independence was declared, and they took their station among the sovereign powers of the earth. The declaration was a glorious document. Sages admired it, and the patriotic of

Henry H. Garnett

every nation reverenced the God-like sentiments which it contained. When the power of Government returned to their hands, did they emancipate the slaves? No; they rather added new links to our chains. Were they ignorant of the principles of Liberty? Certainly they were not. The sentiments of their revolutionary orators fell in burning eloquence upon their hearts, and with one voice they cried, Liberty or Death. Oh what a sentence was that! It ran from soul to soul like electric fire, and nerved the arm of thousands to fight in the holy cause of Freedom. Among the diversity of opinions that are entertained in regard to physical resistance, there are but a few found to gainstay that stern delcaration. We are among those who do not...

"In every man's mind the good seeds of liberty are planted, and he who brings his fellow down so low as to

Peter Salem (left) kills the British Major Pitcairn (center) at the Battle of Bunker Hill.

40

make him contented with a condition of slavery, commits the highest crime against God and man. Brethren, your oppressors aim to do this. They endeavor to make you as much like brutes as possible. When they have blinded the eyes of your mind—when they have embittered the sweet waters of life—then, and not till then, has American slavery done its perfect work...

"Brethern, it is as wrong for your lordly oppressors to keep you in slavery, as it was for the man thief to steal our ancestors from the coast of Africa. You should therefore now use the same manner of resistance, as would have been just in our ancestors when the bloody foot-prints of the first remorseless soul-thief was placed upon the shores of our fatherland. The humblest peasant is as free in the sight of God as the proudest monarch that ever swayed a sceptre....

"Think of the undying glory that hangs around the ancient name of Africa—...

"You had better all die—*die immediately,* than live slaves and entail your wretchedness upon your posterity. If you would be free in this generation, here is your only hope. However much you and all of us may desire it, there is not much hope of redemption without the shedding of blood. If you must bleed, let it all come at once—rather *die freemen, than live to be slaves.* It is impossible like the children of Israel, to make a grand exodus from the land of bondage. The Pharaohs are on both sides of the blood-red waters! You cannot move *en masse,* to the dominions of the British Queen—nor can you pass through Florida and overrun Texas, and at last find peace in Mexico. The propagators of American slavery are spending their blood and treasure, that they may plant the black flag in the heart of Mexico and riot in the halls of Montezumas...

"In 1882, Denmark Veazie (Vesey), of South Carolina, formed a plan for the liberation of his fellow men. In the whole history of human efforts to overthrow slavery, a more complicated and tremendous plan was never formed....

"The patriotic Nathaniel Turner followed Denmark

The death of Captain Ferrer and his crew during the slave rebellion, led by Joseph Cinque, aboard the Amistan, off the Cuban coast, July, 1839.

Veazie (Vesey). He was goaded to desperation by wrong and injustice. By despotism, his name has been recorded on the list of infamy, and future generations will remember him among the noble and brave.

"Next arose the immortal Joseph Cinque, the hero of the *Amistad.* He was a native African, and by the help of God he emancipated a whole shipload of his fellow men on the high seas....

"Next arose Madison Washington that bright star of freedom, and took his station in the constellation of true heroism. He was a slave on board the brig *Creole,* of Richmond, bound to New Orleans, that great slave mart, with a hundred and four (sic) others. Nineteen struck for liberty or death. But one life was taken, and the whole were emancipated, and the vessel was carried into Nassau, New Providence. . . .

"Brethren, arise, arise! Strike for your lives and liberties. Now is the day and the hour. Let every slave throughout the land do this, and the days of slavery are numbered. You cannot be more oppressed than you have been—you cannot suffer greater cruelties than you have already. *Rather die freemen than live to be slaves.* Remember that you are *FOUR MILLIONS!* . . .

"Where is the blood of your fathers? Has it all run out of your veins? Awake, awake; millions of voices are calling you! Your dead fathers speak to you from their graves. Heaven, as with a voice of thunder, calls on you to arise from the dust.

"Let your motto be resistance! *resistance! RESIST-ANCE!* No oppressed people have ever secured their liberty without resistance. What kind of resistance you had better make, you must decide by the circumstances that surround you, and according to the suggestion of expediency. . . ."

Garnet's *Call to Rebellion* is self-explanatory. It is a brilliant achievement, which needs no further amplification. Instead, we will present a few additional excerpts from the address, which contain elements of comparison between the black people's struggle for national liberation and the American Revolutionary War of 1776:

"You will *not* be compelled to spend much time in order to become inured to hardships. From the first moment that you breathed the air of heaven, you have been accustomed to nothing but hardships. The heroes of the American Revolution were never put upon harder fare than a peck of corn and a few herrings. . . . Your sternest energies have been beaten out upon the anvil of severe trial. Slavery has done this, to make you subservient, to its own purposes; but it has done more than this, it has prepared you for any emergency. . .

"Fellow men! . . . behold your dearest rights crushed to the earth! See your sons murdered, and your wives, moth-

Led by a courageous black woman, named Ann Wood, a group of
well-armed slaves escaped by wagon from Virginia, on Christmas
Eve, 1855. Surrounded by a posse in Maryland, Ann Wood, holding
"a double barrelled pistol in one hand and a long dirk knife in the
other, utterly unterrified and full ready for a death struggle," dared
the whites to fire. Instead, the posse beat a hasty retreat and these
proud black folks reached Philadelphia safety.

ers and sisters doomed to prostitution. In the name of
merciful God, and by all that life is worth, let it no longer
be a debatable question whether it is better to choose
Liberty or death."[17]

GARNET'S RESPONSE TO ABOLITIONISTS

Garnet came under attack from the white Abolitionists as a
result of his *Call to Rebellion.* One such attack appeared in *The
Liberator,* which was run by the white Abolitionist William
Lloyd Garrison. In Garrison's absence, the paper was edited by
an Abolitionist poet and writer, Mrs. Maria Weston Chapman.
She condemned Garnet's address in terms which exposed her

white supremist mentality. Garnet sent a sharp reply to her in the form of a letter from his home in Troy, New York, November 17, 1843. Here are excerpts:

"Respected Madam: Some time ago you wrote an article in the *Liberator,* condemnatory of the National Convention of colored people, which was held in the city of Buffalo, in the month of August last... I was born in slavery, and have escaped, to tell you, and others, what the monster has done, and is still doing. It, therefore, astonished me to think that you should desire to sink me again to the condition of a *slave*, by forcing me to think just as you do. My crime is, that I have dared to think, and act, contrary to your opinion... If it has come to this, that I must think and act as you do, because you are an Abolitionist, or be exterminated by your thunder, then I do not hesitate to say that your abolitionism is abject slavery. Were I a slave of the Hon. George McDuffie, or John C. Calhou, I would not be required to do anything more than to think and act as I might be commanded. I will not be a slave to any person or party...

"...the address to the slaves you seem to doom to the most fiery trials. And yet, Madam, you have not seen that address—you have merely *heard* of it; nevertheless, you criticized it very severely. You speak, at length, of myself, the author of the paper. You say that I 'have received bad counsel.' You are not the only person who has told your humble servant that his humble productions have been produced by the 'counsel' of some Anglo-Saxon. I have expected no more from ignorant slaveholders and their apologists, but I really looked for better things from Mrs. Maria W. Chapman, an antislavery poetess, and editor *pro tem* of the Boston *Liberator.* I can think on the subject of human rights without 'counsel,' either from the men of the West, or the women of the East. My address was read to but two persons, previous to its presentation at Buffalo. One was a colored brother, who did not give me a single word of counsel, and the other was my wife; and if she did counsel me, it is no matter, for 'we twain are one flesh.' In a few days I hope to publish the address, then you can judge how much treason there is in it. In the

Nat Turner urging the slaves to rebellion in 1831.

meantime, be assured that there is one black American who dares to speak boldly on the subject of universal liberty."[18]

BLACK RESPONSE TO GARNET'S CALL

From the very emergence of revolutionary nationalism, which can be dated as far back as 1829 when that great revolutionary nationalist, David Walker, issued his appeal to rebellion (*Walker's Appeal*), the white Abolitionists stood in firm opposition. They believed that the black man should remain non-resistant (non-violent), abide by "law and order," and depend upon an appeal to the "tender mercies" of the oppressor (moral suasion). Moreover, the white Abolitionists believed that the black man should follow *their* lead in all matters. Those who didn't were bad "niggers." The emergence of revolutionary nationalism undermined the corrupt role of these white liberal managers in black conventions and in other gatherings of black people.

The *Michigan Negro Convention* held in Detroit on October 26-27, 1843, reflected the growing revolutionary nationalist influence by including in its *Convention Call* the following excerpts which appear to have been taken right out of Garnet's *Call:*

"... For as we are an oppressed people wishing to be free, we must evidently follow the examples of the oppressed nations that have preceded us: for history informs us that the liberties of an oppressed people are obtained only in proportion to their own exertions in their cause. Therefore, in accordance with this truth, let us come up, and, like the oppressed people of England, Ireland and Scotland, band ourselves together and wage unceasing war against the high-handed wrongs of the hideous monster Tyranny....

"Then, come, dear brethren,
  If we would be free,
We must demand our Liberty,
  And strike the blow with all our might,
For Liberty is the Balm of Life."[19]

The *State Convention of Ohio Negroes* met in Columbus, January 10-13, 1849, with 41 delegates, under the leadership of the black revolutionary nationalist, Charles Henry Langston, and others. It was of particular importance in showing the influence of revolutionary nationalism because it dealt a direct blow to white liberal managership. White Abolitionists like Harriet Beecher Stowe and Benjamin Lundy, who have previously been mentioned in regard to their presence or influence at National Negro Conventions, believed that the black man should be gradually and voluntarily emancipated and then returned to Africa or colonized somewhere else. A great section of the white Abolitionists shared these views and they were also the views of Abraham Lincoln. These so-called "friends" of the

Harriet Tubman

In 1851, a black Vigilance Committee in Christiana, Pennsylvania, drove off slave-catchers, killing two members of the posse who had attempted to claim two runaways.

black man were in essence more rabid racists than the promoters of the *American Colonization Society*. The *American Colonization Society* wanted to get rid of the free blacks in order to make slavery more secure. It was clearly a matter of dollars and cents with them. The white Abolitionist supporters of colonization wanted to banish the black man entirely. We will hear more about this later, but first, here are a few revealing resolutions from the Ohio convention of 1849:

"1. To sternly resist, by all the means which the God of Nations has placed in our power, every form of oppression or proscription attempted to be imposed upon us, in consequence of our condition or color....

"6. *Resolved*, That we will never submit to the system of Colonization to any part of the world, in or out of the United States; and we say once for all, to those soliciting us, that all their appeals to us are in vain; our minds are made up to remain in the United States, and contend for our rights at all hazards....

"12. *Resolved*, That we still adhere to the doctrine of urging the slave to leave immediately with his hoe on his shoulder, for a land of liberty, and would accordingly recommend that five hundred copies of Walker's Appeal, and Henry H. Garnet's Address to the Slaves be obtained in the name of the Convention, and gratuitously circulated....

"29. *Whereas* we believe in the principle that who would be free, himself must strike the blow; and

"*Whereas*, Liberty is comparatively worth nothing to the oppressed, without effort on their part, therefore

"*Resolved*, That we recommend to our brethren throughout the Union, that they, thanking their white friends for all action put forth in our behalf, pursue an independent course, relying only on the right of their cause and the God of Freedom...."[20]

LETTER TO AMERICAN SLAVES, 1850

A convention of fugitive slaves was held in September, 1850, in Cazenovia, New York. This convention adopted a document called *Letter to the American Slaves*. This is one of the most important documents in the annals of black revolutionary nationalism. There is no doubt that, destitute as they were in the northern "land of freedom," these fugitive slaves were heavily dependent upon white Abolitionists for economic aid. A few were influenced by the philosophy of these Abolitionists. Therefore, this document not only shows the influence of revolutionary natonalism on this body of black people, but their "tongue in cheek" subtle con-demnation of the white Abolitionist. It is a perfect example of how revolutionary nationalism undermined the foul role of the Abolitionists. Here are excerpts:

"...The Abolitionists act the part of friends and brothers to us; and our only complaint against them is, that there are so few of them. The Abolitionist, on whom it is safe to rely, are, almost all of them, members of the American Anti-Slavery Society, or of the Liberty Party. There are other Abolitionists; but most of them are grossly inconsistent; and, hence, not entirely trustworthy Abolitionists. So inconsistent are they, as to vote for anti-Abolitionists for civil rulers, and to acknowledge the obligation of laws, which they themselves interpret to be pro-slavery....

"The priests and churches of the North are, with comparatively few exceptions, in league with the priests and churches of the South; and this, of itself, is sufficient to account for the fact, that a caste-religion and a Negro-pew are found at the North, as well as at the South. The politicians and political parties of the North are connected with the politicians and political parties of the South; and hence, the political arrangements and interests of the North, as well as its ecclesiastical arrangements and interests, are adverse to the colored population....

"Nevertheless, we are poor, we can do little more to promote your deliverance than pray for it to the God of the oppressed. We will do what we can to supply you with pocket compasses. In dark nights, when his good guiding star is hidden from the flying slave, a pocket compass greatly facilitates his exodus. Besides, that we are too poor to furnish you with deadly weapons, candor requires the admission, that some of us would not furnish them, if we could; for some of us have become non-resistants, and have discarded the use of these weapons: and would say to you: 'love your enemies; do good to them, which hate you; bless them that curse you; and pray for them, which despitefully use you.' Such of us would be glad to be able to say, that all the colored men of the North are non-resistants. But, in point of fact, it is only a handful of them, who are. When the insurrection of the Southern slaves shall take place, as take place it will unless speedily prevented by voluntary emancipation, the great mass of colored men of the North, however much to the grief of any of us, will be found by your side, with deep-stored and long-accumulated revenge in their hearts, and with death-dealing weapons in their hands. It is not to be disguised, that a colored man is as much disposed, as a white man, to resist, even into death, those who oppress him. The colored American, for the sake of relieving his colored brethen, would no more hesitate to shoot an American slaveholder, than would a white American, for the sake of delivering his white brother, hesitate to shoot an Algerine slaveholder. The State motto of Virginia, 'Death to Tyrants,' is as well the black man's, as the white man's motto. We tell you these things not to encourage, or justify, your resort to physical force; but, simply, that you may know, be it your joy or sorrow to know it, what your Northern colored brethren are, in these important respects. This truth you are entitled to know, however the knowledge of it may affect you, and however you may act, in view of it.

"We have said, that some of us are non-resistants. But while such would dissuade you from all violence toward the slaveholder, let it not be supposed, that they regard it as guiltier than those strifes, which even good men are wont to justify. If the American revolutionists had excuse for shedding but one drop of blood, then have the American slaves excuse for making blood to flow 'even unto the horsebridles.'

"Numerous as are the escapes from slavery, they would be far more so, were you not embarrassed by your misin-

Heeding the admonition of a convention of fugitive slaves, that "it is your duty to take the fleetest" of "your master's horses," a slave gallops to freedom.

terpretations of the rights of property. You hesitate to take even the dullest of your masters' horses—whereas it is your duty to take the fleetest. Your consciences suggest doubts, whether in quitting your bondage, you are at liberty to put in your packs what you need of food and clothing. But were you better informed, you would not scruple to break your masters' locks, and take all their money. You are taught to respect the rights of property. But, no such rights belong to the slaveholding community, the rights of property all center in them, whose coerced and unrequited toil has created the wealth, in which their oppressors riot. Moreover, if your oppressors have rights of property, you, at least, are exempt from all obligation to respect them. For you are prisoners of war, in an enemy's country—of a war, too, that is unrivalled for its injustice, cruelty, meanness: and therefore, by all the rules of war, you have the fullest liberty to plunder, burn, and kill, as you may have occasion to do to promote your escape....

"And now brethren, we close this letter with assuring you that we do not, cannot forget you. You are ever in our minds, our hearts, our prayers. Perhaps you are fearing that the free colored people of the United States will suffer themselves to be carried away from you by the American Colonization Society. Fear it not. In vain is it, that this greatest and most malignant enemy of the African race is now busy devising new plans, and is seeking the aid of Government to perpetuate your enslavement. It wants us away from your side that you may be kept in ignorance. But we will remain by your side to enlighten you. It wants us away from your side, that you may be contented. But we will remain by your side, to keep you, and make you more discontented. It wants us away from your side to the end, that your unsuccored and conscious helplessness may make you the easier and surer prey of your oppressor. But we will remain by your side to sympathize with you and cheer you, and give you the help of our rapidly swelling numbers. The land of our enslaved brethren is our land, and death alone shall part us.

"We cannot forget you, brethren, for we know your sufferings, and we know your sufferings, because we know from experience what it is to be an American slave. So galling was our bondage, that to escape from it, we suffered the loss of all things, and braved every peril, and endured every hardship. Some of us left parents, some wives, some children. Some of us were wounded with guns and dogs, as we fled.... and should death itself prove to be the price of our endeavor after freedom, what would that be but a welcome release to men, who had all their lifetime, been killed every day, and 'killed all the day long.'"[21]

Need we comment on the power of revolutionary nationalism as revealed in this document? What appears to be a matter of advice is in reality a matter of advocacy, properly worded so as to satisfy the protocol of paying token homage to the concept of non-resistance. These fugitive slaves looked forward to the "insurrection" of the southern slaves. They provided the justification for a revolutionary course ("Death to Tyrants"). They declared that all of the accumulated property of the oppressor was gotten through brutal robbery of the black man, and therefore the black man was the only one who could claim title to that land and property. They provided revolutionary nationalism with a fundamental understanding of the nature of property under the system of slavery. They declared that the black man was a prisoner of war, with the logical extension that the black people were a people at war. From a convention of fugitive slaves who declared that they represented twenty thousand in Canada, and many more thousands in the free states, and who began their letter with the words, *Afflicted and beloved Brothers,"* came forth a document of magnificent importance.

BALLOTS OR BULLETS

The conventions of Ohio black people became a veritable stronghold of revolutionary nationalist influence. The *Ohio Convention of Negro Men,* held at Columbus City Hall, January 16-18, 1856, indicated what the revolutionary nationalist program held for the "free" North and Ohio in particular. Here are excerpts from the Convention's address to the Ohio State Legislature in which the bold revolutionary nationalist warning stands out clearly:

"... We ask you to ponder the danger of circumscribing the great doctrines of human equality... to the narrow bounds of races or nations. All men are by nature equal, and have inalienable rights, or none have. We beg you to reflect how insecure your own and the liberties of your posterity would be by the admission of such a rule of construing the rights of men. Another nation or race may displace you, as you have displaced nations and races; and the injustice you teach, they may execute; perchance they may better the instruction. Remember, in your pride of race and power....

"Now, admitted that we are men, how are we to *defend* and protect life, liberty and property? The whites of the State, through the ballot-box, can do these things peacefully; but we, by the organic law of the State, are prevented from defending those precious rights by any other than violent means. For the same document that asserts our right to defend life, liberty and property, strips us of the power to do so otherwise than by violence. We ask you gentlemen, in the name of justice, shall this stand as the judgment of the State of Ohio?...

"If we are deprived of education, of equal political privileges, still subjected to the same depressing influences under which we now suffer, the natural consequences will follow; and the State, for her planting of injustice, will reap her harvest of sorrow.... She will contain within her limits a discontented population—dissatisfied, estranged —ready to welcome any revolution or invasion as a relief, for they can lose nothing and gain much...."[22]

ROCK'S DECLARATION, 1858

Dr. John S. Rock, whom we have previously quoted and identified as a distinguished black doctor and lawyer, was one of the most brilliant minds of his generation. His wit, satire and knowledge of history were almost unmatched. During a speech he delivered at Boston on March 5, 1858 (at a meeting commemorating the Boston Massacre), he displayed his revolutionary nationalist influence in a brilliant defense of the black masses against the charge that the black man was a coward.

"White Americans have taken great pains to try to prove that we are cowards. We are often insulted with the assertion, that if we had had the courage of the Indians or the white man, we would never have submitted to be slaves. I ask if Indians and white men have never been slaves? The white man tested the Indian's courage here when he had his organized armies, his battle-grounds, his places of retreat, with everything to hope for and everything to lose. The position of the African slave has been very different. Seized a prisoner of war, unarmed, bound hand and foot, and conveyed to a distant country among what to him were worse than cannibals; brutally beaten, half-starved, closely watched by armed men, with no means of knowing their own strength or the strength of their enemies, with no weapons, and without a probability of success.... take a man, armed or unarmed, from his home, his country, or his friends, and place him among savages, and who is he that would not make good his retreat?...

"The courage of the Anglo-Saxon is best illustrated in his treatment of the Negro. A score or two of them can pounce upon a poor Negro, tie and beat him, and then call him a coward because he submits. Many of their most brilliant victories have been achieved in the same manner. But the greatest battles which they have fought have been upon paper. We can easily account for this; their trumpeteer is dead. He died when they used to be exposed for sale in the Roman market, about the time that Cicero cautioned his friend Atticus not to buy them, on account of their stupidity. A little more than half a century ago, this race, in connection with their Celtic neighbors, who have long been considered (by themselves, of course,) the bravest soldiers in the world, so far forgot themselves, as to attack a few cowardly stupid Negro slaves, who, according to their accounts, had not sense enough to go to bed. And what was the result? Why, sir, the Negroes drove them out from the island like so many sheep,...*

"The black man is not a coward. The history of the bloody struggles for freedom in Hayti, in which the blacks whipped the French and the English, and gained their independence, in spite of the perfidy of that villainous First Consul, will be a lasting refutation of the malicious aspersions of our enemies. The history of the struggles for the liberty of the United States ought to silence every American calumniator....

"The white man contradicts himself who says, that if he were in our situation, he would throw off the yoke. Thirty millions of white men of this proud Caucasian race are at this moment held as slaves, and bought and sold with horses and cattle. The iron heel of oppression grinds the masses of all the European races to the dust.** They suffer every kind of oppression, and no one dares to open his mouth to protest against it. Even in the Southern portion

* The Haitian Revolution of 1793.
** The various brutal European monarchies and despotisms of that period.

In August 1791, a half million black slaves and thousands of free blacks, under Toussaint L'Ouverture, rose up against their French masters, and defeated the French, Spanish and English armies, in order to win independence for Haiti.

of this boasted land of liberty, no white man dares advocate so much of the Declaration of Independence as declares that 'all men are created free and equal, and have an inalienable right ot life, liberty,' &c.

"White men have no room to taunt us with tamely submitting. If they were black men, they would work wonders; but, as white men, they can do nothing. 'O, Consistency, thou art a jewel!'

"Now, it would not be surprising if the brutal treatment which we have received for the past two centuries should have crushed our spirits. But this is not the case. Nothing but a superior force keeps us down. And when I see the slaves rising up by hundreds annually, in the majesty of human nature, bidding defiance to every slave code and its penalties, making the issue Canada or death, and that too while they are closely watched by paid men armed with pistols, clubs and bowie-knives, with the army and navy of this great Model Republic arrayed against them, I am disposed to ask if the charge of cowardice does not come with ill-grace...

"I do not envy the white American the little liberty which he enjoys. It is his right, and he ought to have it. I wish him success, though I do not think he deserves it. But I would have all men free. We have had much sad experience in this country, and it would be strange indeed if we do not profit by some of the lessons which we have so dearly paid for. Sooner or later, the clashing of arms will be heard in this country... 150,000 freemen capable of bearing arms, and not all cowards and fools, and three quarter of a million slaves, wild with the enthusiasm caused by the dawn of the glorious opportunity of being able to strike a genuine blow for freedom, will be a power which white men will be 'bound to respect.' Will the blacks fight? Of course they will. The black man will never be neutral.... Judge Taney may outlaw us; Caleb Cushing may show the depravity of his heart by abusing us; and this wicked government may oppress us; but the black man will live when Judge Taney, Caleb Cushing and this wicked government are no more. White men may despise, ridicule, slander and abuse us; they may seek as they

A large band of fugitive slaves escaping from the Eastern Shore of Maryland.

always have done to divide us, and make us feel degraded; but no man shall cause me to turn my back upon my race....

"The prejudice which some white men have, or affected to have, against my color gives me no pain. If any man does not fancy my color, that is his business, and I shall not meddle with it. I shall give myself no trouble because he lacks good taste....

"I would have you understand, that I not only love my race, but am pleased with my color; and while many colored persons may feel degraded by being called Negroes, and wish to be classed among other races more favored, I shall feel it my duty, my pleasure and my pride, to concentrate my feeble efforts in elevating to a fair position a race to which I am especially identified by feelings and by blood...."[23]

REMOND'S APPEAL, 1858

The spirit of revolutionary nationalism spread everywhere. It even touched black men who had previously espoused the white Abolitionist's corrupt doctrine. At a State Convention of Massachusetts Negroes, which met in the New Bedford City Hall the first week of August, 1858, Charles L. Remond, a noted black anti-slavery orator, urged the black people to embrace a revolutionary course. Here are excerpts taken from a verbatim report of the proceedings by an observer:

"C.L. Remond regretted that he was obliged to ask for rights which every pale-faced vagabond from across the water could almost at once enjoy. He did not go so far as Uncle Tom, and kiss the hand that smote him. He didn't believe in such a Christianity. He didn't object to the (Dred Scott) 'decision,' and the slave bill, any more than to the treatment of the colored race in Iowa and Kansas. The exodus for the colored men of this country is over the Constitution and through the Union. He referred to parties, and asked what either of them had done for freedom. The free-soil and republican parties had, alike, been false. We must depend upon our own self-reliance. If we recommend to the slaves in South Carolina to rise in rebellion, it

John S. Rock

Charles Lenox Remond

Toussaint Louverture

Nat Turner

61

would work greater things than we imagine. If some black Archimedes does not soon arise with his lever, then will there spring up some black William Wallace with his claymore, for the freedom of the black race. He boldly proclaimed himself a traitor to the government and the Union, so long as his rights were denied him for no fault of his own.... Were there a thunderbolt of God which he could invoke to bring destruction upon this nation, he would gladly do it....

"Mr. Remond moved that a committee of five be appointed to prepare an address suggesting to the slaves at the South to create an insurrection. He said he knew his resolution was in one sense revolutionary, and in another, treason-able, but so he meant it. He doubted whether it would be carried. But he didn't want to see people shake their heads, as he did see them on the platform, and turn pale, but to rise and talk. He wanted to see the half-way fellows take themselves away, and leave the field to men who would encourage their brethren at the South to rise with bowie-knife and revolver and musket.

"...He had counted the cost. If he had one hundred relations at the South, he would rather see them die today, than to live in bondage. He would rather stand over their graves, than feel that any pale-faced scoundrel might violate his mother or his sister at pleasure. He only regretted that he had not a spear with which he could transfix all the slaveholders at once. To the devil with the slaveholders! Give him liberty, or give him death. The insurrection could be accomplished as quick as thought, and the glorious result would be instantaneously attained.

"A vote was taken, and the motion was lost. This was by far the most spirited discussion of the Convention."[24]

ROCK'S DECLARACTION ON THE
NATURE OF BLACK CAPTIVITY, 1862

During the second year of the Civil War, Dr. John S. Rock delivered a speech at the annual meeting of the *Massachusetts Anti-Slavery Society,* which exposed the fundamental roots of black captivity in America. This brilliant address speaks for itself.

"This nation is mad. In its devoted attachment to the Negro, it has run crazy after him, (laughter,) and now, having caught him, hangs on with a deadly grasp, and says to him, with more earnestness and pathos than Ruth expressed to Naomi, 'Where thou goest, I will go; where thou lodgest, I will lodge; thy people shall be my people, and thy God my God.' (Laughter and Applause.)...

"The educated and wealthy class despise the Negro, because they have robbed him of his hard earnings, or, at least, have got rich off the fruits of his labor; and they believe if he gets his freedom, their fountain will be dried up, and they will be obliged to seek business in a new channel. Their 'occupation will be gone.' The lowest class hate him because he is poor, as they are, and he is a competitor with them for the same labor. The poor ignorant white man, who does not understand that the interest of the laboring classes is mutual, argues in this wise: 'Here is so much labor to be performed,—that Negro does it. If he was gone, I should have his place.' The rich and the poor are both prejudiced from interest, and not because they entertain vague notions of justice and humanity....

"Our humane political philosophers are puzzled to know what would become of the slaves if they were emancipated! The idea seems to prevail that the poor things would suffer, if robbed of the glorious privileges they now enjoy! If they could not be flogged, half-starved, and work to support in ease and luxury those who have never waived an opportunity to outrage and wrong them, they would pine away and die! Do you imagine that the Negro can live outside of slavery? Of course, now, they can take care of themselves and their masters too; but if you give them their liberty, must they not suffer? (Laughter and applause.) Have you never been able to see through all this? Have you not observed that the location of this organ of sympathy is in the pocket of the slaveholder and the man who shares in the profits of slave labor? Of course you have; and pity those men who have lived upon their ill-gotten wealth. You know, if they do not have somebody to work for them, they must leave their gilded *salons,* and take off their coats and roll up their sleeves, and take their chances among the *live* men of the world. This, you are aware, these respectable gentlemen will not do, for they have been so long accustomed to live by robbing and cheating the Negro, that they are sworn never to work while they can live by plunder. (Applause.)...

"Many of those who advocate emancipation as a military necessity seem puzzled to know what is best to be done with the slave, if he is set at liberty. Colonization in Africa, Hayti, Florida and South America are favorite theories with many well-informed persons. This is really interesting! No wonder Europe does not sympathize with you. You are the only people, claiming to be civilized, who take away the rights of those whose color differs from your own. If you find that you cannot rob the Negro of his labor and of himself, you will banish him! What a sublime idea! You are certainly a great people! What is your plea? Why, that the slaveholders will not permit us to live among them as freemen, and that the air of Northern latitudes is not good for us! Let me tell you, my friends, *the slaveholders are not the men we dread!* (hear, hear.) They do not desire to have us removed. The Northern pro-slavery men have done the free people of color tenfold more injury than the Southern slave-holders. (Hear, hear.) In the South, it is simply a question of dollars and cents. The slaveholder cares no more for you than he does for me. They enslave their own children, and sell them, and they would as soon enslave white men as black men. The secret of the slaveholder's attachment to slavery is to be found in the dollar, and *that* he is determined to get without working for it. There is no prejudice against color among the slave holders. Their social system and one million of mulattoes are facts which no arguments can demolish. (Applause.)....

"When the orange is squeezed, we throw it aside. (Laughter.) The black man is a good fellow while he is a slave, and toils for nothing, but the moment he claims his own flesh and blood and bones, he is a most obnoxious creature, and there is a proposition to get rid of him! He is happy while he remains a poor, degraded ignorant slave, without even the right to his own offspring. While in this condition, the master can ride in the same carriage, sleep in the same bed, and nurse from the same bosom. But give this same slave the right to use his own legs, his hands, his body and his mind, and this happy and desirable creature is instantly transformed into a miserable and loathsome wretch, fit only to be colonized somewhere near the mountains of the moon, or eternally banished from the presence of all civilized beings. You must not lose sight of the fact that it is the emancipated slave and the free colored man whom it is proposed to remove—not the slave; this country and climate are perfectly adapted to Negro slavery; it is the free black that the air is not good for! What an idea! A country good for slavery, and not good for freedom!....

"I do not regard this trying hour as a darkness. The war that has been waged on us for more than two centuries has opened our eyes and caused us to form alliances, so that instead of acting on the defensive, we are now prepared to attack the enemy. This is simply a change of tactics. I think I see the finger of God in all this. Yes, *there* is the hand-writing on the wall: *I come not to bring peace, but the sword. Break every yoke, and let the oppressed go free. I have heard the groans of my people, and am come down to deliver them!* (Loud and long-continued applause.)...

"It is true the Government is but little more anti-slavery now than it was at the commencement of the war; but while fighting for its own existence, it has been obliged to take slavery by the throat, and sooner or later *must* choke her to death. (Loud applause.)..."[25]

BLACK REVOLUTIONARY NATIONALISM VS. BLACK ZIONISM

Not only did revolutionary nationalism undermine the authority and influence of the white liberal managers, but it also dealt a damaging blow to black zionism. Black zionism could only satisfy the greedy ambitions of unprincipled opportunists, who were willing to sacrifice the interests of the enslaved black masses. Revolutionary nationalism had history on its side, and it corresponded to the most vital interests of the black masses. Black zionists cried long and loud about the rape of black women, the murder and plunder of black manhood, and the barbarian, racist cruelty of the oppressor. And their charges were true. But the black zionists were willing to leave their mothers to the lust of the oppressor. They were willing to abandon the enslaved black masses in order to seek their fortune in Africa or wherever else they hoped to find the promised land. Need we raise the question as to the true depth of their concern, or the real measure of their sincerity? Did they merely berate the crimes of the oppressor, as a buying and selling point to put gold and glory in their own pocket? Afro-American history has put a judgement upon black zionism—a judgement from which it cannot escape no matter when or where, or in what new form, it might raise its head. It may flourish for a time, but it cannot escape that judgement.

An example of the defeats suffered by the black zionists during the period under consideration can be found in the proceedings of the *Emigration Convention,* held in Cleveland, Ohio, August 24-26, 1854. We have previously made reference to the speech made by the black zionist, H. Ford Douglass, at this convention. It was revolutionary nationalism which won the day at the Convention as the following excerpts from the *Platform: or Declaration of Sentiments of the Cleveland Convention* demonstrate:

> "Whereas, for years the Colored People of the United States have been looking, hoping and waiting in expecta-

tion of realizing the blessings of Civil Liberty; and Whereas, during this long, tedious and anxious period, they have been depending upon their white fellow-countrymen to effect for them this desirable end but instead of which they have met with disappointment, discouragement and degradation; and Whereas, no people can ever attain to the elevated position of freemen, who are totally or partially ignorant of the constituent elements of Political Liberty; and

"Whereas, in the multitude of Conventions heretofore held by our fathers and contemporaries among the colored people of the United States, no such principles as a basis have ever been adduced or demonstrated to us as a guide for action; and

"Whereas, no people can maintain their freedom without an interested motive and a union of sentiment, as a rule of action and nucleus to hold them together; and

"Whereas, all of the Conventions heretofore held by the whites in this country, of whatever political pretensions— whether Democrat, Whig or Free Democracy—all have thrown themselves upon the declaration: 'To sustain the Constitution as our forefathers *understood* it, and the *Union as they formed it*,' all of which plainly and boldly imply, unrestricted liberty to the whites, and the right to hold the blacks in slavery and degradation.

"Therefore, as the Declaration of Sentiments and Platform of the Convention, be it—

"Resolved,

"1.—That we acknowledge the natural equality of the Human Race.

"2.—That man is by nature free, and cannot be enslaved, except by injustice and oppression.

"3.—That the right to breathe the Air and *use* the Soil on which the Creator has placed us, is co-inherent with the birth of man, and coeval with his existence; consequently, whatever interferes with this sacred inheritance, is the joint ally of Slavery, and at war against the just decree of Heaven. Hence, man cannot be independent without *pos-*

sessing the land on which he resides.

"4.—That whatever interferes with the natural rights of man, should meet from him with adequate resistance.

"5.—That, under no circumstances, let the consequences be as they may, will we ever submit to enslavement, let the power that attempts it, emanate from whatever source it will.

"6.—That no man can have political liberty without the sovereign right to exercise a freeman's will.

"7.—That no individual is politically *free* who is deprived of the right of self representation. . . .

"11.—That a people who are *liable*, under any pretext or circumstances whatever, to enslavement by the laws of a country, cannot be free in that country, because the rights of a freeman necessarily are sacred and inviolable. . . .

"14.—That the political distinctions in many of the States, made by the whites, and accepted of by the colored people, comprise, in many instances, our greatest social curses, and tend more than any thing else to divide our interests and make us indifferent to each other's welfare.

"15.—That we pledge our integrity to use all honorable means, to unite us, as one people, on this continent. . . .

"17.—That the Act of Congress of 1850, known as the Fugitive Bill, we declare to be a general law, tending to the virtual enslavement of every colored person in the United States; and consequently we abhor its existence, dispute its authority, refuse submission to its provisions and hold it in a state of the most contemptuous abrogation.

"18.—That, as a people, we will never be satisfied nor contented until we occupy a position where we are acknowledged a necessary *constituent* in the *ruling element* of the country in which we live.

"19.—That no oppressed people have ever obtained their rights by voluntary acts of generosity on the part of their oppressors.

"20.—That it is futile hope on our part to expect such

good results through the agency of moral goodness on the part of our white American oppressors.

"21.—That all great achievements by the Anglo-Saxon race have been accomplished through the agency of self-interest.

"22.—That the liberty of a people is always insecure who have not absolute control of their own political destiny.

"23.—That if we desire liberty, it can only be obtained at the price which others have paid for it.

"24.—That we are willing to pay that price, *let the cost be what it may.*

"25.—That according to the present social system of civilized society, the equality of persons is only recognized by their equality of attainments,—as with individuals, so is it with classes and communities;—therefore, we impress on the colored races throughout this Continent and the world, the necessity of having their children and themselves properly qualified in *every* respectable vocation pertaining to the Industrial and Wealth accumulating occupations; of arts, science, trades and professions; of agriculture, commerce and manufactures, so as to equal in *position* the leading characters and nations of the earth, without which we cannot, at best, but occupy a position of subserviency.

"26.—That the potency and respectability of a nation or people, depends entirely upon the position of their women, therefore, it is essential to our elevation that the female portion of our children be instructed in all the arts and sciences pertaining to the highest civilization.

"27.—That we will forever discountenance all invidious distinctions among us.

"28.—That no people, as such, can ever attain to greatness who lose their identity, as they must rise entirely upon their own native merits.

"29.—That we shall ever cherish our identity of origin and race, as preferable, in our estimation, to any other people.

"30.—That the relative terms Negro, African, Black, Colored and Mulatto, when applied to us, shall ever be held with the same respect and pride; and synonymous with the terms, Caucasian, White, Anglo-Saxon and European, when applied to that class of people...."[26]

Nowhere in the entire document was there a word mentioned about emigration to Africa or anywhere else. Instead, this document is a brilliant statement of some of the fundamental concepts of revolutionary nationalism. What remains of the black zionist influence is its valuable theoretical contributions to the national question.

Most of the precepts advanced in this document are self-evident. Number 3 states, in effect, that a nation must *possess* the land on which it resides in order to be sovereign. Number 11 states that no black man is free as long as some black men are enslaved. Number 15 unequivocally states that the black people must be united as one force on *this* continent (not Africa!). Number 18 states that the black nation must be represented in a national capacity. Numbers 19-21 give the reasons for the necessity of revolution. Number 19 is a statement of the black nation's need for self-determination. Numbers 23-24 are statements of the necessity of revolution and the determination to pursue such a course. Number 25 reflects aspirations for black capitalism. The rest is self-evident. From the concepts of a nation and national character come the concepts of identity, historical pride, and national unity.

The distance between America and Africa turned many sincere, would-be followers of black zionism into revolutionary nationalists. It seems that it was easier to fight than to swim. Moreover, if America belonged to anyone, it belonged to the black man. As the revolutionary nationalist, David Walker, put it in his appeal to revolution in 1829 (*Walker's Appeal*):

"...Fear not the number and education of our *enemies,* against whom we shall have to contend for our lawful right.... Let no man of us budge one step, and let slave-holders come to beat us from our country. America is more our country, than it is the whites—we have enriched it with our *blood and tears.* The greatest riches in all America have arisen from our blood and tears:—and will

Boston Decr 7th 1831

WALKER'S

APPEAL,

IN FOUR ARTICLES;

TOGETHER WITH

A PREAMBLE,

TO THE

COLOURED CITIZENS OF THE WORLD,

BUT IN PARTICULAR, AND VERY EXPRESSLY, TO THOSE OF

THE UNITED STATES OF AMERICA,

WRITTEN IN BOSTON, STATE OF MASSACHUSETTS,
SEPTEMBER 28, 1829.

THIRD AND LAST EDITION,
WITH ADDITIONAL NOTES, CORRECTIONS, &c.

Boston:
REVISED AND PUBLISHED BY DAVID WALKER.
. . . .
1830.

Title page from Walker's Appeal.

they drive us from our property and homes, which we have earned with our *blood?* They must look sharp or this very thing will bring swift destruction upon them. The Americans have got so fat on our blood and groans, that they have almost forgotten the God of armies. But let them go on...."

THREE ROADS

There were other fundamental differences between the reformists, black zionists, and revolutionary nationalists, which must be reviewed before we close the present chapter. At a State Convention of Ohio Negroes, held in Columbus, Ohio, January 15-18, 1851, a hot debate developed, ostensibly over the Constitution of the United States. The three black men who participated in this debate were H. Ford Douglass (black zionist), William Howard Day (reformist), and Charles H. Langston (revolutionary nationalist). The debate arose over a proposed resolution by H. Ford Douglass, to the effect that no black man could consistently vote under the United States Constitution, because it was a pro-slavery document. But what was really at issue in this debate were the fundamental differences between the three political tendencies. As we shall demonstrate, after presentation of the document, the debate on the Constitution was merely a vehicle to air their differences. Here are excerpts:

H. Ford Douglass

"A Resolution was introduced by H. Ford Douglass: 'That it is the opinion of this Convention, that no colored man can consistently vote under the United States Constituion.'—He spoke for it as follows: Mr. Chairman—I am in favor of the adoption of the resolution. I hold, sir, that the Constitution of the United States is pro-slavery, considered so by those who framed it, and construed to that end ever since its adoption. It is well known that in 1787, in the Convention that framed the Constitution, there was considerable discussion on the subject of slavery. South Carolina and Georgia refused to come into the Union, without the Convention would allow the continuation of the Slave Trade for twenty years. According to the demands of these two States, the

Convention submitted to that guilty contract, and declared that the Slave Trade should not be prohibited prior to 1808. Here we see them engrafting into the Constitution, a clause legalizing and protecting one of the vilest systems of wrong ever invented by the cupidity and avarice of man. And by virtue of that agreement, our citizens went to the shores of Africa, and there seized upon the rude barbarian, as he strolled unconscious of impending danger, amid his native forests, as free as the winds that beat on his native shores. Here, we see them dragging these bleeding victims to the slave-ship by virtue of that instrument, compelling them to endure all the horrors of the 'middle passage,' until they arrived at this asylum of western Liberty, where they were doomed to perpetual chains. Now, I hold, in view of this fact, no colored man can consistently vote under the United States Constitution. That instrument also provides for the return of fugitive slaves. And, sir, one of the greatest lights now adorning the galaxy of American Literature, declares that the 'Fugitive Law' is in accordance with that stipulation; a law unequaled in the worst days of Roman despotism, and unparalled in the annals of heathen jurisprudence. You might search the pages of history in vain, to find a more striking exemplification of the compound of all villainies!..."

Howard Day

"...I cannot sit still, while this resolution is pending, and by my silence acquiesce in it. For all who have known me for years past, know that to the principle of the resolution I am, on principle opposed. The remarks of the gentleman from Cuyahoga (Mr. Douglass), it seems to me, partake of the error of many others who discuss this question, namely, of making the *construction* of the Constitution of the United States, the same as the Constitution itself. There is no dispute between us in regard to the pro-slavery action of this government, nor any doubt in our minds in regard to the aid which the Supreme Court of the United States has given to Slavery, and by their unjust and, according to their own rules, illegal decisions; but *that* is not the Constitution—they are not that under which I vote.... Our business is with the Constitution. If it says it was framed to 'establish justice,' it, of course, is opposed to injustice; if it says plainly no person shall be deprived of 'life, *liberty*, or property, without due process of law,'—I suppose it means it, and I shall avail myself of the benefit of it. Sir, coming up as I do, in the midst of three millions of men in chains, and five hundred thousand only half free, I consider every instrument precious which guarantees to me liberty. I consider the Constitution the foundation of American liberties, and wrapping myself in the flag of the nation, I would plant myself upon that Constitution, and using the weapons they have given me, I would appeal to the American people for the rights thus guaranteed.

"Mr. Douglass replied by saying—

"The gentleman may wrap the stars and stripes of his country around him forty times, if possible, and with the Declaration of Independence in one hand, and the Constitution of our common country in the other, may seat himself under the shadow of the frowning monument of Bunker Hill, and if the slave holder under the Constitution, and with the 'Fugitive Bill,' doesn't find you, then there doesn't exist a Constitution....'

C.H. Langston

"...I perfectly agree with the gentleman from Cuyahoga, (Mr. Douglass) who presented this resolution, that the United States' Constitution is pro-slavery. It was made to foster and uphold that abominable, vampirish and bloody system of American slavery. The highest judicial tribunals of the country have so decided. Members, while in the Convention and on returning to their constituents, declared that Slavery was one of the interests sought to be protected by the Constitution. It was so understood and so administered all over the country. But whether the Constitution is pro-slavery, and whether colored men 'can consistently vote under that Constitution,' are two very distinct questions; and while I would answer the former in the affirmative, I would not, like the gentleman from Cuyahoga, answer the latter in the negative. I would vote under the United States Constitution on the same principle, (circumstances being favorable) that I would call on every slave, from Maryland to Texas, to arise and asset their *liberties,* and cut their masters' throats if they attempt again to reduce them to slavery. Whether or not this principle is correct, an impartial posterity and the Judge of the Universe shall decide.

"Sir, I have long since adopted as my God, the freedom of the colored people of the United States, and my religion, to do anything that will effect that object—however much it may differ from the precepts taught in the Bible, such as 'Whosoever shall smite thee on thy right cheek, turn to him the other also'; or 'Love your enemies; bless them that curse you, and pray for them that despitefully use you and persecute you.' Those are the lessons taught us by the religion of our white brethren, when they are free and we are slaves; but when their enslavement is attempted, then 'Resistance to Tyranny is obedience to God.' This doctrine is equally true in regard to colored men as white men."[27]

H. Ford Douglass was a brilliant man and a superb debater. All one can say about his assertions regarding the Constitution is: "True! true! true!" But the fact remains that black zionists, like Douglass, used these arguments because they did not believe in political action. They were geared to convincing free blacks that they should emigrate from the U.S. and establish a black nation in Africa. Political action requires some measure of hope in the possibilities of improving one's condition under present circumstances. The black zionists could not afford to endorse such an outlook because it contradicted their contention that black liberation is impossible in America, and that the oppressor is eternal. Why bother to patch up a house when you plan to leave it? A fundamental characteristic of black zionism is its opposition, not just to voting, but to almost all forms of political action.

The reformist, William H. Day, on the other hand, presented the absurd view that the Constitution stands above the men who wrote it and who are responsible for its application. He presented the Constitution as some kind of holy scripture, which stands eternally above men and beyond reproach. He said that it is better than the men who wrote it. H. Ford Douglass' reply to Day was not only brilliant, but also brought this reformist back down to the dirty earth upon which the U.S. government stood. Day revealed his typical subservient reformist mentality when he asserted, in effect, that he would act only within the bounds of "law and order" which were established by the Constitution. Political action on a reformist level was *all* he believed in. The reformists did not believe in the revolutionary potential of the enslaved black masses. They were led by the nose by their white liberal managers. They would not violate the "law and order" under which millions of black people were brutally held in chains, by resorting to revolution. They would only play the game by the rules set up by the oppressor. Revolution was good enough for Day's white liberal managers in 1776, but not for the black man who languished under conditions far worse than those which caused the American Revolution.

The black reformists and their white liberal managers called upon black people to wrap themselves in the American flag and to servilely obey and respect the laws of the oppressor. The oppressor's law was written on a blood-stained American dollar bill,´called the Constitution of the United States. Its integrity was monetary and varied only according to the oppressor's need to keep its profit value up, at the expense of the captive black masses. The reformists were in love with this *greenback* Constitution. Pull the master's coat, beg him—whisper, squeak, and scream in his ear about the evils of slavery, but, by all means, kiss the American flag and obey his laws! All of this, while slavery was the law of the land, and the American flag was the banner of slaveholders. Had these Uncle Tom reformists been alive during the American Revolution of 1776, they would have been called Loyalists or Tories and either imprisoned, shot as traitors, or forced to flee the country. The only black men that the oppressor wanted around when he was fighting his own Revolutionary War against England were those who could carry a gun for him, or those who could be his slaves.

The revolutionary nationalists viewed all political action from a revolutionary perspective. A revolutionary struggle for black liberation was their goal. Revolution was their ultimate means. Wherever political action helped to consolidate the black masses, through agitation, demonstrations, voting, etc., it served as an aid to their main object. But they did not believe that voting, on the part of the handful of blacks who could vote, would achieve black liberation. They maintained an over-all revolutionary perspective, while at the same time utilizing political action to achieve certain immediate ends. Charles H. Langston made it amply clear that the first order of business was black liberation, and that he would not be confined within the law and order of the oppressor. Revolutionary nationalists obviously believed that revolution was the highest form of political action that the enslaved black masses could engage in. For them it was merely a continuation of politics by other means. It was not the Constitution of the United States which would decide the ultimate conflict between the oppressor and the oppressed; only the revolutionary power of the enslaved masses could decide this. Power is law. The American revolutionaries of 1776 knew this, and that is why they didn't bother to take their case to King George's courts of law. The black revolutionary nationalists also knew this and it would have made little sense to take the case of black liberation to the U.S. Supreme Court which had time and time again upheld slavery.

The black revolutionary nationalists asserted that the oppressor had no laws that black men were bound to respect, except where such obedience served the convenience of aiding the revolutionary overthrow of the enemy. The slaveholder had no rights that the slave was bound to respect. Temporary and partial, *tactical* obedience to the oppressor's law, under specific conditions of struggle at certain times and places, was advocated as revolutionary expedience dictated. Therefore, the revolutionary nationalists would engage in open, legal, political struggle, where possible, to achieve certain intermediate aims (mainly the consolidation of forces) related to the armed revolutionary overthrow of the oppressor. They had no illusions about voting or talking slavery out of existence. Political agitation and struggle heightened revolutionary potential, and provided the black masses with a weapon more powerful than ten thousand guns. When one understands why it is necessary to go to war in order to achieve liberation, then securing guns and ammunition is only a logical extension of this understanding. Political understanding and organization are more fundamental to revolutionary struggle than the gun. The man is more important than the weapon. *A war of national liberation is merely the continuation of the political understanding of the oppressed masses by revolutionary means.*

Reread the introduction of the *Declaration of Sentiments* of the Cleveland Convention of 1854. The primacy of political understanding is stated: "...Whereas, no people can ever attain to the elevated position of freemen, who are totally or partially ignorant of the constituent elements of Political Liberty;..." etc. This revolutionary nationalist document is no less than a declaration of war, and the guiding political principles are clearly stated. We might call this document the *Black Declaration of Independence.*

FOOTNOTES

1. Woodson, C.G. and Wesley, C.H., *The Negro in Our History* (Washington, D.C., 1922), p. 69.

2. Ibid., pp. 246-247. See also Woodson's *Free Negro Owners of Slaves in the United States in 1830.*

3. *The Liberator,* October 22, 1831.

4. John Brown was not alone in taking a principled revolutionary position on the question of slavery. Other whites (Wendell Phillips, Gerrit Smith, etc.), comprising a mere handful of those known as radicals or abolitionists, assumed a revolutionary position towards slavery. However, the vast majority of abolitionists were white supremists and opportunists of one sort or another. They were the political ancestors of the present-day white liberal managers.

5. *The Liberator,* September 22, 1832.

6. *Proceedings of the Colored National Convention, held in Rochester, July 6th, 7th, and 8th, 1853* (Rochester, 1853, printed at the office of Frederick Douglass' paper).

7. *The Colored American* (N.Y.), October 4, 1837; published in C.B. Woodson, ed., *Negro Orators,* pp. 86-92.

8. *The Negro in Our History, op. cit.,* p. 380. Also see Carl Sandburg's *Abraham Lincoln* (N.Y. 1939), especially pp. 53, 90, 103, 110, 118-119, 212, 330, 345 46, for Lincoln's views on slavery and the black man.

9. *Minutes of the Fourth Annual Convention, for the improvement of the free people of colour...* (N.Y. 1834, pub. by order of the convention).

10. *The Liberator,* March 5, 1852.

11. *Ibid.,* March 12, 1858.

12. *Proceedings of a convention of the Colored Men of Ohio, held in the City of Cincinnati, on the 23rd, 24th, 25th and 26th days of November, 1858* (Cincinnati, 1858).

13. *Proceedings of the Colored National Convention held in Rochester, 1853, op. cit.*

14. *Ibid.*

15. *Op. cit., The Negro in Our History,* p. 493.

16. *Proceedings of the National Emigration Convention of Colored People; held at Cleveland, Ohio... 24-26 August, 1854* (Pittsburgh, 1954).

17. *A Memorial Discourse; by Rev. Henry Highland Garnet, delivered in the Hall of the House of Representatives, Washington... February 12, 1865, with an introduction by James McCune Smith* (Phila., 1865), pp. 44-51.

18. *The Liberator*, December 3, 1843.

19. *Minutes of the State Convention of the Colored Citizens of the State of Michigan, for the purpose of considering their moral & political conditions, as citizens of the State* (Detroit, 1843). Copy in the Boston Athenaeum.

20. *State Convention of the Colored Citizens of Ohio, convened at Columbus, January 10-13, 1849* (Oberlin, 1849).

21. Salem, Ohio, *Anti-Slavery Bugle*, September 28, 1850; published by Helen Boardman in *Common Ground* (Spring 1947), vol. VII.

22. *Proceedings of the State Convention of Colored Men, Held in the City of Columbus, Ohio, January 16th, 17th, and 18th, 1856* (n.p., n.d.).

23. *The Liberator*, March 12, 1858.

24. *Ibid.*, August 13, 1858.

25. *Ibid.*, February 14, 1862; indications of audience response are from original.

26. *Proceedings of the National Emigration Convention of Colored People, 1854, op. cit.*

27. *Minutes of the State Convention of the Colored Citizens of Ohio, convened at Columbus, January 15-18, 1851 (Columbus, 1851).*

NOTE

Excerpts containing much of the documentation used in this study can be found in *A Documentary History of the Negro People in the United States,* edited by Herbert Aptheker, with a preface by W.E.B. DuBois (N.Y., 1962). The introductory matter which precedes each excerpt in Aptheker's book is often misleading and, perhaps, in certain cases, reflects the editor's own political aberration. He makes no clear delineation between reformism, black zionism or revolutionary nationalism. He gives the impression that the term "Abolitionist" embraced such people as Martin R. Delany, H.H. Garnet and others who represented very distinct and fundamentally different political trends, and who can in no way be lumped together with the white Abolitionists.

Martin R. Delany was not an Abolitionist. He did not believe that slavery could or would be abolished in the United States. H.H. Garnet was not an Abolitionist; he was a revolutionary nationalist. In his introductory note on page 363, concerning the Cleveland Emigration Convention of 1854, Aptheker says, "Noteworthy in this convention was the expression of a feeling of and a yearning for Negro nationality." Thus, he dismisses this extremely important document with an obscure bit of understatement.

The documents in Aptheker's book can only be understood in the context of an independent study of Afro-American history.